DAUGHTER

of the

WHITE RIVER

DAUGHTER
of the
WHITE RIVER

Depression–Era Treachery &
Vengeance in the Arkansas Delta

DENISE WHITE PARKINSON
Foreword by Dale P. Woodiel

THE
Hi§tory
PRESS

Published by The History Press
Charleston, SC 29403
www.historypress.net

First published 2013
Second printing 2014

Manufactured in the United States

ISBN 978.1.60949.913.6

Library of Congress CIP data applied for.

For my children: Jasper Williams, Grace Norton and Cason Parkinson.
Love is real, not fade away.

...the tragedy began
With Homer that was a blind man,
And Helen has all living hearts betrayed.

—W.B. Yeats

Contents

Foreword, by Dale P. Woodiel   11
Preface   13
Acknowledgements   17
Introduction   19

Chapter 1. Childhood and School Days   27
Chapter 2. Don't Call Me a River Rat   33
Chapter 3. Moonshine, Outlaws and the Younger Gang   40
Chapter 4. Depression-Era Treachery   46
Chapter 5. "She Showed No Remorse"   53
Chapter 6. A Chance at Liberty   59
Chapter 7. Trapped in Hell   65
Chapter 8. A Series of Daring Escapes   71
Chapter 9. Betrayed by the State   77
Chapter 10. A Reckoning   85
Chapter 11. Forget Me Not   93

Epilogue   99
About the Author   101

Foreword

Although black-and-white box cameras were common in the 1930s even in relatively isolated river communities like Crockett's Bluff, it would have hardly occurred to someone to make a picture of the five or six houseboats moored (or tied up) along the mile or so bank of the White River between the bluffs themselves and the next bend to the north just past what I recall as a favorite sandbar for swimming in the late 1940s.

The Woodiel house rested on a modest rise above the bluff overlooking the river, but many of my parents' friends lived literally on the river in houseboats, which generally floated on great logs. Among my earliest childhood memories is a visit to the houseboat of Mr. and Mrs. George Gosnell, during which time Mr. Gosnell, to my great delight, allowed me to choose an apple from a large barrel-like container. Years later, the Gosnells moved to a house on land a few hundred yards northward up the riverbank across from the Marrs family.

There was another occasion, when I accompanied my father on a winter afternoon visit, during which he and Mr. Gosnell smoked corncob pipes filled with raw tobacco roughly ground from complete tobacco leaves that I believe he ordered by mail from Kentucky. Although the fumes from their pipes brought tears to my youthful eyes, the stories they exchanged made it worth the discomfort.

It might well have been on such a visit that I first heard the tale—at the time still fresh in the minds of river folks—of a woman "who went right into the DeWitt Court House and shot a man dead" before she was sent to prison and later killed trying to escape.

The details as well as the sentiments of this story were renewed afresh when I received a request from Denise Parkinson to use a watercolor image of a houseboat from the "Crockett's Bluff" website, which I've nurtured for the past few years, devoted to the preservation of the culture of this place along the river where I was born. Our correspondence revealed her plans for *Daughter of the White River*, the focus of which is Helen Spence, the woman of the tale from my childhood.

Stories emerge from generation to generation the way wildflowers burst forth season after season without any special consideration from those who are stunned by their seasonal emergence. So it is with the stories that continue to emerge from the culture that thrived along the lower White River in Arkansas during the 1920s and '30s, when the area was alive with communities of families. The river was their fundamental life source, a world whereby through hunting, fishing and mussel shelling they sought and secured their livelihoods from year to year, generation to generation.

As Parkinson reveals in this sensitive and enlightening recollection of one of its major legends, it was an isolated and independent world with its own sense of community and its own concepts of love, responsibility and justice—essentials of all enduring cultures.

Ancient verities worthy of our consideration in any season.

DALE P. WOODIEL, 2013
West Hartford, Connecticut

Preface

Ifirst wrote about my childhood memories of the White River more than a decade ago for the *Arkansas Democrat-Gazette* newspaper. The short piece provided filler for a weekend section in the promotions department where I was employed as an editor.

I had traveled to the upper reaches of the White River, to the tiny town of Possum Grape, by way of even tinier Grande Glaise (or the other way around) for a separate feature story. Some nice folks showed me staggering piles of mussel shells left over from early twentieth-century button factories. They also brought out a collection of nineteenth-century French coins excavated from the riverbanks. Grande Glaise is named for its fine clay, dug and exported by long-ago French explorers.

I wish I had a copy of what I wrote then. The pages got lost along the way. My journalistic efforts and travels compose a disappearing study of vanishing customs, artifacts, people and places. This sympathy began when I witnessed firsthand the loss of our family home (actually an ancient houseboat situated on land) and property on the banks of the White River, a river I initially thought was named after our family (the Whites) due to the logic of childhood.

Our summer place near Clarendon was where I saw, up close, my first cicada and alligator gar. Food tasted better there; sleep was deeper. I heard my first ghost story there, sitting around the campfire listening to my father and grandfather describe mysterious lights on the river that followed them one night when they were running trotlines. Our summers on the White came to an end in the late 1960s when the U.S. Army Corps of Engineers suddenly and arbitrarily manipulated the river's water level.

On the subject of the Army Corps of Engineers that built "the Dam" that caused the change in water levels of the White River and subtracted the home and summers of living outdoors, fishing every day and generally enjoying everything, my father could rage and sometimes did. But the damage was done. The old homeplace was underwater. And no amount of car trips to randomly identical Official Arkansas State Park campsites, with their concrete picnic tables on slabs and tents like refugee camps beside murky lakes trapped behind cement walls…none of the manufactured Great Outdoors could atone for the loss, a loss that over time went unspoken. (Clarendon, I knew thee not.)

This catalogue of loss multiplied throughout families like ours who had, for generations, kept houseboats, hunted and fished, never bowing to overseer or landlord. The numbers of people forced off the White River swelled, marking the disintegration of community across an entire region. Sons, daughters, siblings and cousins dispersed, moving away from one another and the river, away from land and family at an equal pace of subtraction.

At the height of the Great Depression, Congress made the lower White River a National Wildlife Refuge, but there was no refuge for the River People when the richest bottomland was placed off-limits. The pattern of leaving accelerated during and after World War II but went deeper than mobilization. River People were not—we were not—"Owners." The Owners were fewer and farther between. And as towns dwindled and annual Reunions ceased, as work dried up, debts mounted, marriages splintered and children gave up more than what the parents had together, the disintegration spread in a wave that caught my family, too, with imploding results.

After a nomadic lifestyle, I returned to Arkansas to settle in Hot Springs. I met a variety of people; Hot Springs attracts nomads from all over the world thanks to its famous healing waters. I heard of an old-timer in town who knew a lot about the White River. Not waiting for an introduction, I looked him up in the phone book and called him right away. Meeting L.C. Brown was like finding a long-lost cousin—an octogenarian cousin with a knack for storytelling. I listened to his stories of the White River. He spoke of his childhood friend, Helen Spence, with a mixture of pride and pain.

Helen Ruth Spence was beloved by the River People for her beauty and kindness. But when her father was murdered, the young girl did not hesitate to avenge his death. When she smuggled a pistol into the courtroom and shot her father's killer in front of judge, jury and spectators, Helen unleashed a chain of events that sealed her fate. Her brutal murder spawned headlines across the nation, yet she was forgotten, her grave unmarked. There had to be more to this story.

I began researching in order to piece together a biography for the *Encyclopedia of Arkansas History and Culture*. Some published articles suggested that Helen spent her early childhood in Clarendon—my lost ancestral home. Newspaper headlines from the Flood of 1927 throughout the drought years of the Great Depression reflected the current era of the Second Great Depression, in which Arkansas now ranks third in hunger. Despite the differences between then and now—a time before the "consumer economy," before agriculture became agribusiness—similarities prevail. Injustice prevails. H.L. Mencken was right in saying, "So long as the Arkansas of today remains the Arkansas of 40 years ago, the Menckens are going to make it the butt of ridicule, and millions are going to agree with them."

I requested Helen Spence's file from state prison archives, and when a fat envelope arrived in the mail, I rushed to show L.C. Brown. Her prison records, dating from the early 1930s, provide both essential portrait and damning truth: the State of Arkansas was not above torturing or murdering its children.

L.C. Brown's memories add a missing dimension to the tragedy of Helen Spence. The newsmen and editors who splashed her story across front pages and magazine covers wrote in predictably sensationalized, lurid ways. Their Depression-era narrative amounts to little more than character assassination. To the newsmen, she was "great copy," nothing more. But to the River People, the loss of Helen Spence is bound up in the loss of the White River itself, as her exile was ultimately shared by the greater community. For decades, subsequent writers have repeated earlier accounts without delving into existing records of Helen's imprisonment. It is past time for a correction.

By weaving together timelines from official records, double-sourced published accounts and the vivid reminiscences of L.C. Brown, I steered the straightest course I could in writing this book. But just as time is often described in terms of a river, I reached back for help from my own "downstream people" for scenes that needed to be re-created. Thus, the character of Ada Spence is brought to life through the words and actions of my great-grandmother, Altha Ray Wimberly Granberry, widow of riverman Joe Granberry. She lived in a houseboat until she was evicted by the state.

My memories of the White River are few: the shop-fan built into the wall of the bedroom where my sisters and I slept, a constant breeze pouring over layers of quilts; the vibrating chant of frogs, birds and insects; and the red-handled pump in the kitchen where my great-grandmother baked biscuits, a hand-rolled cigarette dangling from her lips.

Heirlooms from my father's side are equally few: a watercolor of a Quapaw brave painted by my late aunt, a fishing knife my grandfather made from airplane parts during World War II and some 8mm home movies. The grainy silent film opens with scenes along the White River. Boats come and go, sunlight filters through tall trees and stringers of fish and bullfrogs dangle from the hands of smiling men, women and children.

I do not know their names.

Acknowledgements

This book would not have been possible without the kindness and encouragement of my buddy, L.C. Brown; the inspiration of my role model, philanthropist Dorothy Morris; the grace of my commissioning editor, Christen Thompson; and the support of my husband, Steve, and family. A special thank-you goes to *Hot Springs Life and Home* magazine and Good Earth Natural Foods of Hot Springs, my family business heroes, for patience, understanding and employment during the writing of this book.

Introduction

Arkansas' White River is a spirited creature, prone to overreaching its banks. Named for foaming rapids along its upper channel, the river springs from Ozark Mountain headwaters. From there, it flows capriciously due north into Missouri, only to turn southward and reenter Arkansas, a territorial name that describes "downstream people": the ancient Quapaw tribe. Twisting below gray bluffs and thick woods, the White River tunnels a green and gradually widening course more than seven hundred miles, while on either side falls away the grand prairie of the Arkansas Delta. Reaching its great conflux, the White merges with the yawning mouths of the Arkansas and Mississippi Rivers. Together, this triune of waters engraves a fluid boundary mapping the southeastern contours of the state.

Like a fecund vein tracing and feeding the earth, the lower White River cuts through fertile bottomland. Here, a jungle of mighty hardwood trees marks the remnant of a primeval forest deep enough to conceal rare birds once believed extinct. Here, too, the river—no less haunted than the forest—is said to harbor in its depths a rarely seen "monster" reminiscent of a distant Loch Ness cousin.

Before it was tamed by man-made monsters—titanic dams built during a wave of mid-twentieth-century engineering—the White River harbored a second wave of downstream people. Hardy settlers came pioneering from the British Isles and Europe, arriving in Arkansas' eastern territory to discover an Eden abandoned by Native Americans banished in the name of progress. Some settlers built houseboats using wide planks of native cypress that silver to a gray sheen in the wind and rain. Floating homes sheltered families who worked and thrived, rocking to sleep each night and waking to the rhythm of the water. The houseboat families married their existence with that of the river at a time when it was a road, before engines and railroads brought the land to bear beneath iron tracks.

Standing apart from the law and beyond the scope of town and city, houseboat communities followed a code of "River Justice." Townsfolk and farmers living away from the water were "dry-landers." City life was then as it is now attuned to the clockwork machinery of money and propriety—twin pillars upholding a system of law wherein justice is mere coincidence.

As freighted keelboats came and went, the settlers remained. When graceful, storied paddle-wheelers and laden barges set out from New Orleans bringing cargo the length of the White River, the settlers were still there. They called themselves "River People," and their youngest and dearest child is a memory that will not die: a girl named Helen Ruth Spence.

Helen Spence has lain for nearly a century in a grave as unmarked as her place in history. But this state of affairs is changing, in accordance with the natural law of the river that makes a constant of change and still rages untamed. Helen was born aboard a houseboat on the White River a few years prior to World War I; the exact date of her birth is unknown. She was the second child of Cicero Spence and a woman named Ellen Woods. Helen's older sibling, Edna, suffered infantile paralysis and never walked. Helen called her sister "Edie," and the two grew even closer after their mother died.

Cicero eventually remarried a woman named Ada. The Spence family became prominent among the Delta's houseboat community. Neighbors sought Cicero for his skill in matters of fishing, hunting and trapping, as well as for his wisdom in resolving disputes. A small, wiry man with a thin, weathered face, Cicero shared his knowledge of the river with his daughter, teaching her as he would a son. Helen learned to shoot a pistol as well as she could sew and to sew as well as she could catch and gut a fish.

Together with her stepmother and Edie, Helen kept a cozy home for her beloved father, bringing his coffee or pipe tobacco when he sat musing on deck after dinner. She delighted in running errands for Cicero. Leaving the moored houseboat to scamper up its wooden stage plank, Helen moved soundlessly through the maze of forest paths. A petite girl, small-boned and lithe but strong, Helen wore dresses of cotton or wool and long johns in place of stockings. Deep brown eyes and delicate cheekbones fringed by dark curls lent an elfin quality to her smile. She often sat in the filtering sunlight with Edie, chattering and singing as they sewed quilt-pieces or mended nets.

Toward sundown, Helen helped Ada cook—during summer in pots set out of doors, during winter in the houseboat's small cast-iron woodstove.

This indoor/outdoor existence moved like a May Day circle-dance from water to land and back. When it was time to make lye soap, hoe the garden patch or feed the chickens strutting about the riverbank, Helen tended her chores quickly so she could tag along with Cicero as he checked his traps and trotlines. The river spilled its bounty: silvery-blue channel catfish; brown mudcats that bark when pulled from the water; fish with long rubbery paddle-shaped noses; buffalo, drum and sharp-toothed alligator gar that shred the seine nets. Overhead, migrating flocks of ducks and geese darkened the skies at midday. And from the hillsides: whitetail deer peering between trees, fat fox squirrels perched like dinner on a limb, thickets full of rabbits and bullfrogs round as skillets. River People fed one another amply from nature's store. They did not hunt for sport, wasted nothing of what they caught and knew of no such word as "poacher." Winking, the River People said, "Hunting season? That's what you use to flavor the meat."

When Helen was old enough to carry the heavy water bucket from the spring, she made it an adventure. The best times to fetch water were sharp, clear mornings that sent shafts of sunlight piercing through the trees. Helen rose in silence, moving carefully from beneath the shared quilt so as not to wake Edie. Barefoot in the dew, with no fear of snakes because of the air's cold bite, she took the narrow, hard-packed dirt pathway to the cold-water spring hidden in the woods not far from where the Spence houseboat was tied. Insects, too groggy and cold to sing, waited as the sun increased. Hidden birds gave voice with trills and clicks. Passing below the rustling canopy of leaves, Helen listened for the giant woodpecker's scream. She arrived at a stand of cottonwoods and stepped forward into the shadowy place near their tangled roots, the spring's home.

The cold spring, an artesian well, was marked and walled by a fifty-five-gallon drum with its bottom cut out. Set deep into the sandy bank like a tube, its metal rim was level with the ground. Lifting the iron lid and peering down into the cylinder, as though looking into a living mirror, made it impossible to gauge the water's depth. The clarity of the surface played tricks on the eye, becoming invisible. At the bottom of the spring, a bed of white-gold sand boiled continually, dancing and spiraling grains sending up fingers from the center of the circle. This water held its own scent, different from the rich smell of the river. The spring's odor conjured splintered ice and caverns of colorful crystals alive and growing, before they erupt to break between the world's crust and the air.

Daily rituals at the heart of river life made each week a series of workdays leading up to Saturday and Sunday. Saturdays meant a trip to the county seat of DeWitt or baseball games and impromptu horseraces at nearby Ethel. Arkansas County is the oldest county in the state. Founded in 1813, Arkansas County is even today made up of small towns and farm communities. During the first half of the twentieth century, most dry-lander communities possessed a mill, a mercantile and a church.

Sundays were for rest and worship. River People regarded religion from a standpoint akin to the Garden of Gethsemane; their Holy Trinity encompassed rake, shovel and hoe. The community's mode of worship centered on Brush Arbors, a shared tradition of the South's African American families. They built ephemeral churches on the spot. Men and women constructed frames of willow and cane, open-air pavilions situated along the river. Branches, leaves and vines twined and piled on the framework, shading the congregation from noonday sun. The river became a baptismal font. At night, the Brush Arbor, strung with lanterns and emanating hymns, filled the riverbank with light and song.

The wheel of the year turned from spring planting season to summer labor, pausing for annual autumn gatherings. Every October, after the crops were gathered in, the community celebrated the harvest with a week of music and feasting. This festival, called simply "the Reunion," attracted Arkansas County families by the wagonload and heralded the approach of Christmas. Drawn by teams of horses or riding in Model T Fords, River People and dry-landers alike arrived at Camp Doughboy, a Veterans of Foreign Wars (VFW) campground south of DeWitt. Anyone carrying a musical instrument got in for free. Dancers crowded a central pavilion that rang with fiddles, banjos and guitars punctuated by the raspy beat of the washboard. Wood fires, roast pigs on spits, fried chicken—cooking smells mingled from scattered booths and tents among the shade trees. A forerunner to the county fair, the Reunion offered a place for women to buy, sell or trade fresh batches of molasses, fruit preserves and honey, while men haggled over saddles and boots. For children, it was a cherished holiday.

North of DeWitt, toward the White River at St. Charles, an older Reunion ground hosted similar festivals. Camp Fagin, established during the Civil War, overlooks Indian Bay. Locals call Indian Bay "Stinking Bay" ever since a cavalry battle there during the Civil War saw countless corpses of soldiers and horses swell the river. A nearby stretch of water marks the sinking of a Union gunboat called the *Mound City*. The gunboat entered the White via the Mississippi at a confluence known as Rivers End. Advancing as far as

St. Charles, the *Mound City* met resistance: a local Confederate militia drove mule teams parallel along both sides of the riverbank, hauling a heavy chain stretched taut across the river. Unable to turn around or back out, the doomed ship became a floating target for a Confederate shore battery. One lucky shot sent a cannonball hurtling down the gunboat's smokestack, exploding the boiler like a bomb. The only monument in St. Charles—a tall stone monolith marking the epicenter of the town's main crossroads—stands in remembrance of this single most destructive shot of the Civil War.

Helen and her playmates knew little of war, although they unearthed musket balls from time to time when digging around on the riverbanks. Their childhood encompassed a lull after the so-called Great War. The "Roaring Twenties" described something taking place in big cities like Memphis and St. Louis. "Jazz Age" was a phrase for the hoo-hah going on in gambling dens of paddle-wheelers or bawdy houses in New Orleans—places whispered about in late-night adult conversations overheard by youngsters eavesdropping from adjacent bedrooms. Children of the White River, untroubled that the nearest movie theater was miles away, had plenty to occupy their senses and did not require entertainment.

St. Charles boasted a post office and several small stores. The town's icehouse occupied a bluff near the outskirts at a steep bend marked by a log chute. Here, loggers rolled timber into the water, huge hardwood trunks lashed together to be taken downriver. But it was mostly fishing and mussel-shelling that occupied the River People. Boats pulled up to the icehouse dock to unload hauls of fish that were weighed, packed on ice in wooden boxes and shipped out. The riverbed sheltered freshwater mussels big as a man's fist. The mussels rested in the current, opening and closing, seining the water. River People steered small wooden shell boats, trolling a line spaced with hooks that caught the mussel by the lip. Mussel shellers walked straight into the river, where shallows and sandbar met. Using a diving helmet crafted from the barrel-shaped gas tank of a Model T, the diver set the metal cylinder on his shoulders and commenced to wade in. Weighed down by the helmet and some rocks, the diver made his descent, dumping rocks as needed to surface again. Some helmets had a window of glass; sometimes the men just moved along blind in the river's murk.

Using a hand pump, the diver's partner forced air through a long hose that fed inside the helmet. Feeling with gloved hands underwater, shellers hauled up stringers of mussels by the thousands. Upriver at Grande Glaise, an old French settlement town, a button factory cut the roseate shells into myriad buttons in an era before plastic. Sometimes a mussel gave up a pale, oblong pearl. People called the pearls "River Tears." Regarded as treasures, the rare freshwater pearls were kept as a reminder that the river could break a human heart. "The river gets its revenge," the people told each other, saying, "The river will eat you up in the end."

One brutal winter saw the White River ice over. The few houseboats equipped with metal hulls were enlisted to break the ice so children could get to school. Drowning was a constant danger even in good weather, for adults as well as children. But the houseboat communities thrived by sharing all of what little they had. Helen was a schoolgirl in 1927 when a massive flood churned the Mississippi into a muddy inland sea. The Great Flood of '27 sent the White River flowing backward. Forests, tilled fields and houses disappeared under an endless lake dotted with treetops and the occasional steeple. Huddled in rows of government-supplied tents, stranded dry-landers waited atop levees for the waters to recede. Livestock that didn't drown had to float or swim. Cows, horses, pigs (and unknown numbers of dead bodies) wedged in trees, on ridgelines and rooftops. Delta families of 1927 witnessed a catastrophe of biblical proportions—although the River People were, like Noah, better prepared for the ordeal.

Local legend holds that one massive flood caused a large, empty, well-made houseboat to float into the tiny Arkansas town of Yancopin, south of St. Charles. The townspeople made it Yancopin's post office. Details of the flood are impossible to confirm; however, the nephew of Yancopin's last postmistress certifies that before it was used as a post office, the landlocked houseboat was a saloon. The houseboat-turned-saloon-turned-post office still stands a century later on a grassy rise, having outlasted the now-deserted town.

Cicero Spence built a fine shanty boat for his family. With a tin roof pitched like a lean-to, the thirty-foot-long wooden structure floated atop two huge cypress logs, pontoon-style. Its gangplank did not lead straight down to the front door, as on other houseboats, but rather to a walkway along the side of the boat, a sort of breezeway outfitted with chairs. Other boats could tie up along that side, and better yet, Ada did not have to suffer people walking through the house. Mosquito netting canopied the beds. The houseboat's several rooms were devoted to cooking, eating, sleeping and gathering before the potbellied stove fire. Light shone from kerosene lanterns—not the fluted glass kind, but metal railroad lanterns that hung from rafters, swaying with the boat's pitch.

On some houseboats, the grandparents papered their bedroom walls with newsprint. At night, dipping snuff, old-timers simply spat onto the wall and tore off the newspaper to dispense with the splatter. The Spence houseboat had screened windows; others boasted glass and still others made do with wooden shutters that folded down when pulled to. "Maw, did you pull the rope?" was a nightly refrain that referred to the houseboat's latch door. Pulling in the rope secured the latch for the night, although there were plenty of lookouts ready to sound alarms along the river, if need be.

The River People designed their own alarm system. They set great store on the skill of whittling, carving cedar "quills" (tiny wooden whistles). No two quills sounded exactly alike. By night, the whistle's pattern alerted the community to intruders or said, "I am here." From darkened hillsides, the calls of night-birds and coyotes mingled with the sounds of coded, musical messages between the River People. Moonshiners, signaling one another from bank to bank, warned of approaching lawmen. Their whiskey stills, hidden in steep tangles, remained undiscovered more often than not.

Like a country unto itself, the White River rose and fell with the seasons until long about the year 1929, when the world intruded with a vengeance. The Delta had survived the Great Flood of '27 when the rivers came together to spread fertile loam on the land, heedless of life or death. Crops and fish and game rebounded—they always had. As the last golden summer of the 1920s waned, the River People of Arkansas found no warning of a coming storm.

Chapter 1

Childhood and School Days

G et in the car, Junior, we're going to the river." These were words Lemuel Cressie Brown Jr. liked to hear, especially on late-summer Sunday afternoons, which tended to bog down. The towheaded youngster, just beginning to lose his baby fat, slammed out the screen door and raced across the dirt yard to the two-door Model A. Shiny black and brand new, the car had instantly supplanted in his affections a formerly beloved cart drawn by the family's pet goat. The boy had moved on. He now considered the goat-cart a mere toy, "baby stuff."

As Lem Brown Sr. pulled away from the family farm and steered down bumpy dirt and gravel onto the two-lane blacktop of Highway 1, Junior looked out the window, chin resting on his bare, tan arm. Cornfields and haystacks flashed by in golden streaks under a blue sky.

"Where we goin', Dad?" Junior asked. "To see Uncle Archie?" He liked visiting Great-Uncle Archie's big old houseboat. "Are we going fishing?" the boy persisted.

"We're paying a visit to Cicero Spence," replied his father. "There's a situation down on the river."

Junior's dad sounded more thoughtful and serious than usual. If he needed to talk to Cicero about something, then it must be important. The boy was proud to be the son of Lemuel Cressie Brown Sr., deputy sheriff of Arkansas County. In this capacity, Sheriff Lem (as he was called) rode out first on a horse and later in a Ford. He came to know most every family in Arkansas County. Sheriff Lem kept his silver star tucked inside his shirt pocket and, unlike other lawmen of his time, was a respected figure due to his understanding of the River People. Whenever anyone on the White River had a court appearance to make, Sheriff Lem would talk to Cicero Spence. Word went out, and the person always showed up to the courthouse in DeWitt on time.

"Is it moonshiners?" Junior blurted. Getting no answer, he went back to staring out the window. A man leading a mule team waved from a dirt road, and the child waved back.

They drove through St. Charles—"just a widenin' in the road"—heading past the icehouse on the bluff. Turning off Highway 1 onto another dirt road, the car finally slowed to a stop. The White was running low after a hot, dry summer; the river lay stretched around a curve, muddy banks and sandbars exposed. Junior counted three herons. A row of flat-shelled turtles stretched nose-to-tail atop a log, sunning. At the base of the bank, Cicero Spence's wooden houseboat floated. It was the color of a papery-gray hornet's nest; its towline was looped around a stob. Hankies fluttered from a wash line tied to one of the eaves.

Overcome by shyness, the boy elected to wait in the car. He watched his father stride to the Spences' stage plank. From his vantage point, Junior could see Cicero sitting on the deck down below. The riverman leaned back in a chair, shotgun across his lap, hat pulled low over his eyes. Sheriff Lem reached the top of the stage plank and paused to tap out his pipe. A loud shot rang out from the houseboat. Startled, Junior ducked. Sheriff Lem kept on filling his pipe as though nothing had happened. The boy edged back up, peeking out of the car. A clump of leaves spiraled down from a cottonwood tree to land at his dad's feet. His father struck a match and lit his pipe.

Cicero laid aside the gun as Sheriff Lem descended to the boat and pulled up a chair. Junior couldn't hear what they were saying. Craning his neck, he looked up and down the length of riverbank. A figure stood waving from a distance—it was Cicero's daughter, Helen Spence. Junior recognized her from the Reunion. Every year, Helen cut a fine figure dancing with her beaux. She beckoned again. Observing his father and Cicero engrossed in conversation, Junior climbed out of the car.

"If it isn't little Lem!" Helen said as he approached.

"They call me Junior Brown," the boy mumbled. Helen took his pudgy hand and gave a firm shake. She had already graduated from school and looked every bit of "sweet sixteen" in her yellow summer frock and straw bonnet. Her stockings were white cotton fishnet.

"You're getting to be so tall!" she cried. "You need a big boy's name. How about L.C.—can I call you L.C. Brown, instead of Junior?"

The child considered for a moment before nodding assent. The two strolled farther along the grassy bank. L.C. looked back to see Ada coming out the door of the houseboat. She was drying her hands on her apron and nodded to him. He waved, slipping his other hand comfortably into Helen's as they walked. Stopping at a shady spot, Helen sat down in a patch of clover, motioning for the boy to sit beside her. For a time, they listened to the water's slow lapping while the sun slanted through the trees—an altogether drowsy day. Helen laughed suddenly, putting a finger to her lips, saying, *shhhhh*! As L.C. watched, she pulled up her skirt a little ways, exposing a roll of $100 bills tucked behind the mesh of white stocking. The boy stared open-mouthed at the wad of cash pressed against her leg.

"Daddy needed a place to hide his money," she said. "That's $300!"

From that moment on, L.C. Brown was in awe of Helen Spence. The two jumped up and ran whooping along the bank down to the mudflats. Everywhere, crawdad mounds stuck out of the moist clay like cypress knees, little brown chimneys that popped up overnight. Aiming straight at the crawdad mounds, L.C. kicked them over one by one, sending clods of mud flying as Helen screamed. The crawdad inside scooted backward, tunneling tail first and claws last into the murky waterhole. The pair played until the evening bats came out. Every time L.C. laughed, Helen would holler, "Your tickle-box tumped over!" which only made them both laugh harder. When dusk fell, his father whistled for him to get in the car.

As the Ford rumbled onto Highway 1, headlights tunneling through the darkness, the boy asked, "Why did Cicero shoot at you?" To which his father replied, "He wasn't shooting at me—he would have hit me if he was. That's just Cicero's way of saying hello."

"Oh. Dad, guess what? Helen doesn't call me Junior. She calls me L.C. Brown."

"That's fine, son."

By the time they reached the house, the child was sound asleep and did not wake when carried upstairs and tucked into bed.

Weeks passed, and school began anew. L.C.'s big brother, John Homer, seven years older, went to school in St. Charles proper, while L.C. cut through fields and woods to get to the schoolhouse at Pleasant Grove, Arkansas. Pleasant Grove was a tiny community with no store, just a Baptist church and a schoolhouse facing each other from opposite sides of the road. Mother packed biscuits and sausage into lunch pails, and the boys set out after a breakfast of eggs, grits and fresh buttermilk. L.C. made certain to use his new name, and the school year got off to a good start. Soon, Saturday dawned in brilliant fall colors, and Sheriff Lem went to visit Cicero Spence. L.C. tagged along, bringing his fishing pole just in case.

When they got to the houseboat, Ada was outside washing clothes. She explained that Helen was walking to the log chute with a friend. L.C.'s dad gave permission for him to go—"but don't get below the tree line"—so the boy dropped his pole and tore off toward the bluff. Coming around a bend, L.C. caught sight of Helen walking with a skinny dark-haired boy. He gave a shout, and the two stopped and turned. It was John Black—his family's houseboat was near to Uncle Archie's. As the trio resumed walking, John explained that a load of hickory was coming in. It was fun to watch the loggers roll timber into the river. The tree trunks thundered down the chute into the water, disappearing completely before popping back to the surface. Then the men made a "tow." Climbing and balancing atop the massive floating trunks, loggers pounded iron railroad spikes into each one and lashed them together with huge chains, ready for the trip downriver to the sawmill.

As the friends reached the log chute, the *Mary Woods* came in sight, blowing its steam whistle. Helen clapped her hands—the big paddle-wheeler was always a sight to behold. People waved from the decks behind white railings as the bright red wheel churned. A load of cotton bales sat stacked on the prow. There came a commotion from the road. Topping the bluff, several men appeared, guiding two log-wagons. Teams of straining horses pulled half a dozen ragged hickory trunks toward the chute. L.C. spotted Buck Joiner, a black man his father knew.

"Howdy Mr. Joiner," he called. "Are you cooking molasses again this year?" (The Joiner family kept a sorghum mill in Pleasant Grove. Keaton Flat was the name of their place, over near Immanuel schoolhouse. Buck was a logger, too.)

The man replied, "Yep, tell your Pa I said hello, and we'll see y'all the middle of October. Good cane crop this year."

Nearby, a sunburned fellow in a greasy hat was barking orders. He was the man in charge of getting the "tie"—the right number of logs to make a tow for the riverboat. The load of hickory was giving him a hard time, and so were the horses. "Kid!" he yelled at L.C. "Get back, kid! You're gonna get hurt!"

"I wanna see 'em float!" the boy retorted, stepping away from the edge of the bluff. "You see that?" L.C. said, and John nodded. Helen asked, "What? See what?"

Buck Joiner walked over to view the spectacle. Pushing against the logs with long poles, the men started the hickory rolling. An avalanche of wood plunged down the chute and into the water with a mighty splash. Everyone stood waiting. L.C. and John burst into hoots of laughter. The logs just sank. Being of a dense and heavy grain, hickory does not float easily. "I told you they wouldn't float that-a-way," Buck Joiner exclaimed. "You need cypress logs in between 'em! A cypress and a hickory, et cetera."

The foreman tore off his hat, throwing it to the ground and unleashing a hail of curses. He sounded like a Yankee, cussing and raising hell. Buck Joiner walked away with the rest of the disgusted crew. The foreman turned a baleful eye on John and L.C. rolling around on the side of the road, gasping with laughter. He started up yelling again; L.C. caught the phrase "damn river rats." Helen snatched a hickory nut off the ground and lobbed it at the Yankee, catching him upside the temple. The three took off running and didn't look back until the houseboat came in sight. Ada was still doing the wash. Chuckling contentedly, the trio fell silent until Helen observed, "What a waste of good hickory."

Sometimes when L.C. accompanied his father to St. Charles, Helen was nowhere to be found. On such days, the boy romped with other children of the river. Several families kept a jumble of houseboats tied up just the other side of the cold-water spring. There, L.C. found a dozen ready playmates. These families—parents, grandparents, aunts and uncles—were all Italians and Germans. None of the adults bothered to speak English. L.C. soon found that if he wanted any dinner, he better say the right words. He got to where he could speak "Eye-talian" and German so well that the old grannies pinched his cheeks and ruffled his thatch of yellow hair. They did not neglect to give him extra helpings.

Once, during lunch in the schoolyard, L.C. heard some older girls talking about Helen. These girls were known gossips and behaved as though they were "the only hogs at the trough." Their fathers owned big tracts of land and worked their tenants ragged. The boy resolved to inquire about what he had overheard the next time he saw Helen.

Ducks and geese began returning to the Delta, and soon Cicero and Sheriff Lem went hunting. "You stay and look after the womenfolk," Cicero ordered, winking at L.C., and the men left, taking an old hound dog with them. The boy sat on the deck of the houseboat with Helen and her sister, Edie, tossing bits of bread into the water. Shoals of bream and minnows fought for the scraps, their bodies flashing silver in the light. After a while, L.C. forgot Edie was there—she sat so quietly, a quilt tucked around her motionless legs.

"Helen," the boy asked suddenly, "what does 'jump the broom' mean?" He had to repeat the question and then tell where he heard the words before she would answer. After Helen graduated ninth grade, a local boy named Buster Eaton had proposed marriage, and she ran off with him. Buster Eaton turned out to be a moonshiner. The marriage lasted only a short while before Helen returned to the river. Throwing her arms around Edie's shoulders, Helen cried, "I'll have no truck with bootleggers!" The sisters hugged each other tight as L.C. looked away. Little fish swirled greedily in the current, chasing dissolving bits of bread.

The night before the trip to Keaton Flat, L.C. could not get to sleep at all. The boy was excited about all the fun he would have at the sorghum-making. A waxing moon shone too bright through his window, so he got up and padded out to the hallway landing. The child lay down on the cool smoothness of the wood floor, resting his chin on his hands. The house was quiet but for the grandfather clock and a distant hum of voices downstairs, which meant that Mother and Dad were up late talking. L.C. listened to his grandparents' soft snores down the hall. His brother slept soundlessly in the room behind. His parents' voices ebbed. The boy caught the words "Black Thursday," but the phrase meant nothing, and sleep soon overtook him.

Chapter 2
Don't Call Me a River Rat

From beyond a rise in the dirt road came the voices, soaring and falling like the song of cicadas. L.C. begged his parents to let him jump down from the buckboard and run on ahead, but Mother insisted he ride up to the Joiners' place together with the family. Jostling beside his big brother in the back of the wagon, L.C. fumed, biding his time.

> *Green Sally up, Green Sally down*
> *Last 'un squat, gotta tear the ground*
> *Old Miss Lucy dead and gone*
> *Left me here to weep and moan...*

Gripping the side of the wagon, the boy scanned the scene as Keaton Flat came into view. The house and outbuildings stood along a ridge overlooking a creek, while gently rolling fields stretched away to the tree line. Turning leaves were still thick on this Indian summer day. Everywhere was bustle and activity: trucks and wagons pulling in, picnic baskets coming out and tents going up. In the distance, the molasses operation was in full swing, wood fire blazing. The late-morning sun glinted off a long table topped by more canning jars than the boy had ever seen. Men and women moved swiftly and efficiently, exchanging or unpacking needful things, talking and laughing.

The young Joiner cousins gathered over by a big oak tree. There were always so many cousins around during the molasses-making that L.C. could hardly keep track. For years, he'd addressed them collectively as "y'all." The buckboard slowed to a stop, and the boy launched over the side and ran toward the group of children.

Green Sally up, Green Sally down
Green Sally baked her possum brown...

Boys and girls stamped their feet in time, dropping low to the ground and rising to clap in syncopation. L.C. joined in the old field holler as a cloud of dust swirled around the chanters:

Old Miss Lucy dead and gone
Left me here to weep and moan
If you hate it fold your arms
If you love it clap your hands.

The songs never had less than ten verses, and when one stopped, another began. The cousins' well ran deep when it came to rhymes and rhythms. One skinny girl brought out two long ropes, and a line of kids formed for double-dutch. The jump-rope rhymes began, and L.C. found a spot in the shade to watch.

Lookee yonder, Black Betty (bam-a-lam)
Jump down, Black Betty (bam-a-lam)
Black Betty had a baby (bam-a-lam)
Li'l thing went crazy...

The ropes swung faster. The two girls doing the jumping focused on nothing but their feet, while the girls in charge of the rope frowned in concentration, lips shut tight and arms arcing like machines. Bare legs pumped in a blur as the chant got louder. L.C. clapped excitedly. Catching sight of Uncle Archie's big bay horse coming up the road, the boy bolted across the meadow to greet him. Uncle Archie rode tall in the saddle—all the Brown family men were over six feet, counting their hats. Swinging a lanky arm, Uncle Archie grabbed L.C. by the jacket and hoisted him up in front. The horse pranced, tossing its mane as the boy held tight to the pommel.

From this height, L.C. could see clumps of pale green cane piled by the settling vat. Cutting sorghum is heavy work; Buck Joiner and his brothers used a grub hoe, stripping the lengths of cane by hand and cutting off the seeds at the top. A mule walked in a circle, turning the metal rods of the grinder. Cane juice gushed noisily through a burlap filter into a bucket. When full, the contents of the bucket went into the cooking vat to settle. The ten-foot-long vat of galvanized tin was pitched with a series of trapdoors that allowed gravity to send the settled juice along its way to be cooked and cooled. Buck and his brothers had risen in the wee hours to build the fire underneath, using fast-burning pine. They were already on their second "run" of sorghum. Clouds of steam billowed from the boiling, foamy green sap. Uncle Archie lifted L.C. down so he could get a closer look and left to tie up the horse.

Buck Joiner stood over the vat, wooden skimmer in hand. He skimmed the juice, studying the color and texture as it dripped. The man's face and arms were shiny with sweat. "It's too stringy," Buck declared, grabbing a ladle and stirring the mixture. Another man placed some more wood on the fire. The cooking down of sorghum is a delicate process—if you don't cook it enough, it sours and ends up as hog feed. If you cook it too much, the syrup scorches and turns to hard sugar. It would take hours for the juice to thicken into dark amber molasses, so L.C. sauntered away.

People stood in small groups or sat in folding chairs, visiting. A table was steadily filling with covered dishes—a potluck. L.C. watched some men play a game of horseshoes until he spotted John Black walking toward the creek, cane pole in hand. L.C. crossed the field to join him. Some kids from Pleasant Grove were already down in the creek. The children greeted John and L.C. with the news that they'd cornered a big snapper.

The turtle, half-buried in the muddy streambed, had been spied by a sharp-eyed youngster. They had set upon it with flat rocks and sticks. After excavating the snapper's pointy gray shell, the children maneuvered the creature into the shallows, where they took turns poking at it. It was as big as an iron skillet, and it being October, the thing was half asleep.

"Leave 'im alone!" a familiar voice rang out, and a dozen heads turned to see Helen Spence. She strode over to where John and L.C. squatted on their hams. "Could you spread out your jacket?" she said. John laid his leather coat on the bank, and Helen plunked down, arranging her skirt. "How can y'all let them torment one of God's creatures?" she challenged.

"My Daddy won't let me shoot anything 'cept we're gonna eat it," L.C. piped up. Helen leaned over and ruffled his hair. Suddenly bashful, the group released its captive. The turtle rose into the current and wobbled off downstream as the children splashed away to find another prospect.

The three companions sat watching the children trudge around a bend. Helen pointed to a sycamore bent low over the water, its crown of leaves turning red-gold. "Can you see—it looks just like a lady with white arms and golden hair," she whispered. They all stared at the tree; John elbowed L.C. conspiratorially.

"That's the ghost tree," John deadpanned. "Buck Joiner told me all about it—walks around at night, under the full moon. Say, there's a full moon tonight, come to think on it." Sunbeams seemed to set the sycamore ablaze.

"I seen fox fire, but not a tree ghost yet," L.C. said solemnly. Helen stood, brushing at her skirt. "Come on, let's go get something to eat," she suggested.

The picnic was spread over half an acre, a fragrant and varied buffet. Platters of fried chicken, squirrel and catfish joined roast venison and pork amid a colorful collection of vegetable dishes—corn, potatoes, fried okra and greens. Fruit pies outnumbered cakes two to one, and each table or picnic blanket held a mound of biscuits and pancakes ready for sorghum molasses. Ladies who prided themselves on their breads and pastries took center stage today. L.C.'s mother liked to whip fresh cream butter into the molasses, his favorite. Folks milled about filling plates and wandered off to sit in the shade. L.C. tagged along with Helen and John, who didn't seem to mind. Near the oak tree, someone had set up a cider press.

"Wanna try some live-apple juice?" a lady asked as L.C. walked by. She handed the boy a little tin cup, and when his face scrunched up, she nodded happily. "Good, ain't it?" she cried. "Arkansas Black apples and Granny Smiths—they came a good crop!"

"Yes ma'am," L.C. gasped, eyes watering. He accepted a piled-high plate from somebody and sat down next to Helen and John. When a mason jar of the new molasses was passed, the boy eagerly poured the syrup over his biscuits. The flaky brown biscuits swam in the molasses, getting drenched and sticky—just the way L.C. liked 'em. The sun slanted lower as grown-ups went back for seconds and children went back for thirds.

Someone brought out a guitar, and instantly L.C. was surrounded by folks pulling harmonicas from pockets and instruments from banged-up cases. One man took a broom-handle strung atop a washtub and played bass. As the afternoon lengthened, the old songs came out one by one, sung by high, reedy voices, with a range of deeper voices chiming in for the chorus. Helen played the spoons for one tune, a song about two sisters walking down a stream—the elder one pushed the younger, fairer sister in to drown. Their beau came along and made a fiddle out of the pretty girl's bones and bowstrings from her long yellow hair. L.C. shivered—cool air was breathing up from the creek. He looked around to see Mother sitting nearby. The suddenly sleepy boy stumbled over and crawled into her lap. The moon rose as another year's sorghum harvest passed into memory.

Whatever the mystery of October is that makes the month so all-fired what-where, it got better every year. After the molasses-making, there's the Reunion and, before you know it, Thanksgiving and Christmas. School recedes awhile. With any luck, there'd come a snowfall, and Mr. Williams would hitch his plow-horses to the sledge, everybody cheering and taking rides. Prospects looked pretty good for an American kid in October 1929.

Whenever L.C. couldn't fall asleep in his bed, he went and stretched out on the hallway landing's wood floor. Sometimes he brought his pillow and blanket. In the morning, he always woke up in bed with no memory of how he got tucked back in. The night before the Reunion, dozing on the landing again, he heard voices from downstairs. It was Mother and Dad at the kitchen table. The voices changed, taking on an urgency and a shrillness—a rarity in the Brown household. The boy propped on his elbows and caught the words "stock market" and something about New York. New York—that was a million miles away! He got up and trotted to the bedroom, trailing his blanket.

"John Homer," he whispered, shaking his brother awake. "Something bad happened at the cattle auction in New York City!" John Homer just shoved at him and rolled over.

"Don't say I didn't warn ya," the child yawned, climbing into bed.

Early next morning, the Browns hitched up the wagon and set off after John Homer milked the cows. Grandma and Grandpa rode in back with the kids—having met at a long-ago Reunion, they made the journey every year. The road to Camp Doughboy was filling up. The procession of trucks, horses and mule-drawn wagons filed through a landscape bursting with autumn—violet sumac against pale, tufted grass; yellow hickories; and oaks and cypress in bright orange hues. Cedars, hollies and pines shone green, and the random pattern covered the land, a crazy-quilt under a perfect sky. L.C.'s mother had made a poem especially for October, so to pass the time she recited it:

> *When the month of October returns*
> *And the days must shorter grow*
> *The leaves on the trees all colors turn*
> *And fall to the ground below*
> *The sumac in gorgeous color bright glows among the trees*
> *Making gloomy corners light as it has for centuries...*

Not to be outdone, Grandpa Homer countered with an old song, one they always sang picking cotton:

Way up 'ere in the mountains in the kingdom of the pine
I lived all alone with this ol' white mule of mine
Back caved in and he's mighty thin
His legs was strong and fine
I sing this song as he carries me along
This ol' white mule of mine.
When they have a dance in the valley
And my work's done at the still
I climb aboard this ol' white mule
And go riding down the hill
When Judgment Day is come
And the golden stairs I climb
I know St. Peter will welcome me
On this ol' white mule of mine.

A hawk turned lazily against the sky. Clouds were moving in from the north, and smoke from occasional chimneys drifted up as the wagon rattled past. When they reached the Reunion grounds, the buzz of the crowd overwhelmed jangling harnesses and rumbling engines. Shouts of recognition and snatches of song flowed past. As soon as the wheels stopped, L.C. vaulted from the wagon and escaped.

After playing red rover awhile, the boy wandered over to the pavilion to watch the musicians tuning up for the dance. They offered him a plate of fried chicken and went back to a spirited discussion.

"I bet you two bits she shows up and puts 'em all to shame," the drummer exclaimed. "I sure do like to see 'er dance."

"Long as it makes you play better," joked another.

"She's a purty li'l thing," mused a mandolin player as the rest of the band murmured in agreement.

"I know who y'all are talking 'bout," L.C. blurted.

"Sonny, don't yack with your mouth full—and no, you do not."

"Oh yes I do!" the boy hollered. The musicians laughed as L.C. ambled away. The boys in the band were not disappointed. After the music started, folks on the dance floor swept aside as Helen entered wearing a red velvet dress. Her skill with a needle and thread was well known; with its velvet cape, white collar and matching rabbit-fur muff, the outfit was a looker. Helen stood smiling and then somebody grabbed her around the waist, and the dancers took off.

The song—a Cajun ditty about if you don't have any crawfish, then you don't eat any crawfish—went 'round and 'round in dizzying loops, as did the couples. Sitting cross-legged on the edge of the dance floor, L.C. watched, coughing in the evening chill. As from a great distance, voices clamored above his head.

"Miz Brown—your boy ain't well!"

"Look at them spots—he's got the hard measles!"

Chairs overturned and people scattered as L.C. was caught up in his father's arms and carried to the wagon. The ride home was a blur of hoof-beats and Grandma Nora praying to the air. For weeks, L.C. lay in bed quarantined, window shades drawn against the light, croup-kettle simmering nearby. John Homer moved his desk and bed downstairs to the sitting room so L.C. could rest. The merest sound jarred the small patient, who held himself as still as he could—even so, after the measles an ear infection took hold with yet more pain. Thanksgiving came and went, unmarked. Entire days revolved around doses of Grandma Nora's senna-leaf tea and remedies made from tree bark and Lord knows what else. His mother hovered nervously, a few times bursting into tears. By Christmastime, the boy was able to sit up in bed.

His father was doing some logging to make ends meet (damn New York cows were causing problems for everybody). Lem Brown came home from the woods one day and rushed upstairs without taking off his coat. "Junior," he called, "I brought you a present!" Reaching inside the coat, his dad drew forth a tiny, squirming ball of dark fur.

"Me and Buck Joiner were cuttin' a tree, and in a hollow was three wolf pups," Lem explained. "This one's the survivor—a male—full-blood timber wolf. See? He's got red eyes."

L.C. nodded weakly and managed a smile. Nestling against each other, boy and wolf pup fell into a deep sleep.

Chapter 3

Moonshine, Outlaws and the Younger Gang

Whan springtime came, it was as though a collective sigh of relief went up to heaven—at least from the Brown household, whose youngest member was finally well again. L.C. had not come through the long winter of illness unscathed, however. The boy looked different—pale, thin and with a darker tint to his hair. He'd also fallen behind in school and grown restless from inactivity and getting fussed over by Mother and Grandma Nora.

L.C. began skipping school every chance he got. The wolf pup accompanied him, a silent shadow. Mornings after they reached the schoolhouse, Wolf hid along the tree line and waited until school let out to follow the boy home. He wasn't like a hunting dog—he never sounded or barked, although he could growl menacingly enough. Wolf took his cues from L.C. Folks stopped referring to the boy as "Sheriff Lem's son" and began calling him "the kid on Big Creek that got the wolf" (Big Creek being a bayou near the Brown farm).

L.C. took to going off squirrel hunting with Wolf, ranging through the woods and swamp between Big Creek to the south and Tarleton Creek to the north. Fox squirrels, red and bushy-tailed and plump, were his prey—the smaller, rat-like gray squirrels that folks call "cat squirrels" were not worth the trouble. The boy was fast becoming a crack shot. His brother had always been the better student; John Homer was also better at milking cows. L.C. usually got the milk pail kicked over and made a mess. So when the child started showing up at the screen door with meat for the table, his mother asked no questions. Money was tight, and it all had something to do with New York City, as Dad and Grandpa Homer kept saying.

Sheriff Lem was restless too, and for reasons beyond the tableau of spring. He began going into St. Charles two or three times a week, picking up supplies "on the ticket" and conversing for hours. L.C. rode along. Wolf, refusing to get in the car, was consigned to the barn; terrified of the creature, Grandma Nora insisted. On the way to town, father and son stopped by the neighbors to ask if they needed anything. By the time Sheriff Lem pulled up to Ballard Dean's Mercantile, there was a tidy list.

"I'll be awhile," he said. "You run along and find your friends."

It was only two hundred yards to the boat landing, and L.C. walked slowly, gulping deep breaths of river-scented air, taking in the countless shades of green coming from all sides. The landscape glistened from an early morning rain shower. A flock of chickens fled noisily before his feet as he neared the Spence houseboat. Helen was coming up the stage plank, a basket on her arm. Shading her eyes with one hand, she hesitated.

"Edie! Ada! It's little L.C. Brown—he got well!" Helen cried, bounding the last few steps to stand beaming down at him. Her dark eyes studied the changes in his face, and L.C. saw tears spring up. She was instantly forgiven for having called him "little." Her hair was streaked with flour. The boy asked, "Is there some kinda pie-making going on?"

Helen's basket was full of early dewberries—even better than blackberries. Blackberries take up half the summer just to get ripe. "The pies are baking right now," Helen explained. "I'm taking the rest of these berries over to Miz Dupslaff—come with me! You speak German, don't you?" Untying her juice-stained apron, she ran her hands through her hair and grabbed a little drawstring purse.

The two took their time walking to the other side of the spring. Along the way, a strategy was devised: they would finagle some of Miz Dupslaff's legendary bread pudding. L.C. was to do all the talking. It was settled: an afternoon of bread pudding and fresh dewberry pie. Maybe pick some flowers for Ada and Edie. Suddenly Helen stopped and spun around. The pair stood stock-still in the empty dirt road.

"Look—goosebumps," the girl muttered, extending her wrist. "Did you hear something?"

L.C. shrugged as Helen shivered again. "When you get a rigor like that, Ada says it's a rabbit runnin' over your grave," she murmured. They continued on.

There was always a gaggle of towheaded kids running around the Dupslaff place, and today was no exception. The youngsters were playing by the garden, while Miz Dupslaff kept an eye on them from her usual spot on the houseboat deck. Seated on a wooden cask, she overflowed her perch in a cascade of shawls, scarves, skirts and apron. Layers of petticoats peeked from underneath. On a card table was a bottle of muscadine wine and tin cup close at hand. She also kept ahold of a green hickory switch—a sort of scepter for commanding the youngsters. Beckoning, she lifted her cup.

The children stood silently by as Helen and L.C. made their way on deck and handed over the basket of dewberries.

"What's she saying?" Helen asked as the woman chattered away in German.

"She's saying she could make wine out of 'em."

"She could make wine out of rainwater," said Helen.

Summoning his sweetest smile, L.C. asked (in German) if there was any leftover bread pudding to be had. The woman patted him on the shoulder, grinning and nodding. Heaving to her feet, she put aside the hickory switch and shuffled through the houseboat doorway. Emerging with plates and utensils, she set these on the card table and went back inside. She returned carrying a trivet and a steaming cup of sauce—the sauce with something in it that turned bread pudding into a magical food. Chuckling, she balanced the cup on the little trivet.

L.C., who could hardly sit still, exclaimed, "When I was sick, I would'a killed for some of Miz Dupslaff's bread pudding!" Helen nodded, observing, "Sickness is a hard master."

Producing a pan half-full of sweet-smelling bread pudding studded with raisins, the woman cut two slabs and drizzled generous amounts of sauce, still chuckling. Helen and L.C. dug in, eyes rolling with pleasure. Miz Dupslaff poured herself another cup of wine, humming in triumph. The group of children edged closer to the plank, never taking their eyes off the bread pudding, and she brandished the hickory switch. "Nein!" she spat.

On the way back home, Helen stopped again in the middle of the road. She listened intently, a frown crinkling her brow. An afternoon breeze sent dust devils whipping along the ground. L.C. demanded to know what in heck was going on, and the girl finally said, "If I tell you, you can't tell anybody." They resumed walking as Helen described how, lately, something had changed. The river was seeing strange people and even stranger happenings. There was a story going around about the *Mary Woods* riverboat and two missing boys from DeWitt. They weren't but a few years older than Helen.

"One night, the two boys were on the *Mary Woods*, drinkin' and gamblin' and carousin'." Helen's voice fell to a whisper. "And they got killed—nobody's seen 'em since."

L.C. pondered this news. "What's 'carousin'?'" he asked.

"I think it's when you get ahold of moonshine and turn jealous and go to fighting," Helen answered. "It's pretty bad. But it gets worse—they say those two dead boys got thrown into the *Mary Woods* furnace and burnt right up!" She leaned in closer, whispering, "You wanna see what I got in the bag?" Loosening the drawstring purse, she held it open, and L.C. peered inside. The purse held a pistol and some bullets.

"It ain't loaded," the girl muttered as the child gawked. The pair had reached the Spences' garden and did not notice L.C.'s dad waiting in the nearby car. His voice caused them both to jump.

"Hello, Miss Helen. Junior, hop in. We got to get home. Looks like a storm brewing."

For days, L.C. could not stop thinking about what Helen said. At night, after the rest of the family was asleep, he'd sneak downstairs and whistle softly for Wolf to come inside. It was against Grandma's orders, but the boy couldn't help it; he liked to dangle his arm over the side of the bed, where his hand could rest against Wolf's warm fur. One night, L.C. hatched a plan that involved skipping school. He would make the trek to the White River on foot. The trick was to start early and get back before sundown with no one the wiser. The next day dawned perfect for such a mission—this was no morning for sitting indoors behind a desk like some broody hen. Grandma Nora nodded in approval when the boy packed extra biscuits and sausage for lunch. He slammed out the screen door and was joined by Wolf gliding close behind. As the house receded from view, the two cut across a cotton field and headed north to St. Charles.

L.C. did not have a gun, but he had his pocketknife and Wolf and so feared nothing. Taking the path through the woods, he stopped to cut a walking stick in case snakes were out early. As the sun climbed higher, the pace grew more leisurely. There was a patch of quicksand along this swampy route, and when they neared the spot, the boy bent some branches to mark it. The mossy ground squished, sucking at his boots. Stopping under a shady oak, L.C. shared some biscuits and sausage with Wolf. Sitting leaned back against the trunk, the boy brushed handfuls of fallen leaves over his legs. Soon he was buried up to his belly. Overhead, a pair of fox squirrels chased each other in noisy spirals around the boughs.

Boy and Wolf grew still, nestled in the cool, damp leaves. A doe appeared, leading her spotted fawn down the path. The deer's big brown eyes glittered. Perking her ears, the doe stopped. L.C. followed her gaze to see something large coming through the woods. The deer turned and were gone. The boy put his hand on Wolf, hardly daring to breathe as a silent figure passed: a broad-shouldered black man well over six feet tall. His sweat-stained leather hat was in tatters, and he wore a buckskin jacket. He carried a tow sack.

After the man was gone, L.C. counted to fifty and jumped up, changing direction. Aiming toward Uncle Archie's the boy hurried, looking over his shoulder more than once. Coming out of the forest behind the icehouse, he saw the *Mary Woods* docked below. L.C. couldn't help staring before ducking behind a tree—a boy playing hooky with a wolf was too noticeable. Seeking a vantage point, he scooted forward on his stomach and peered from beneath some bushes. From the edge of the bluff, he could view people coming and going from the distant riverboat. Wolf lay down as L.C. watched the road.

The sound of breaking twigs and high-pitched laughter startled the boy from a doze. Wolf's fur bristled. Two women were walking in the forest, their voices growing louder before passing beyond the icehouse. They came out of the woods and sashayed across the road to where the paddle-wheeler lay docked. As L.C. stared, a familiar form stepped from the Mercantile, bottle of Coke in hand. It was John Black, and he was headed in this direction! L.C. waited until the right moment and then tossed a handful of pebbles at John's feet.

"Ow! What're you doing there—skipping school? Is that a wolf?" John ran up the steep embankment and squatted on his heels. Chugging half the cold Coke, he handed the bottle to the thirsty boy, and L.C. finished it off, gasping.

After L.C. described the day's adventures, John considered awhile before responding. "I never heard of a black man hiding in the woods," he said slowly. "But those two that went by just now—they's hoors." When L.C. shrugged, John snapped, "If you don't know what a riverboat hoor is, I sure ain't gonna tell ya!"

Standing and scanning the sky, he said in a gentler tone, "If you want to get home without being caught, you'd best hurry."

That night on the porch after dinner, Grandpa Homer told the story of the time he sold a horse to the Younger Gang. L.C. sat cross-legged at his feet—he knew this story but never tired of hearing it. His dad listened from the porch swing, smoking his pipe. Grandpa continued: "This was after they quit running with Quantrill's bushwhackers—there was two of 'em. They were riding double and rode out their horse near Cold Springs. They were going into Louisiana, and I traded 'em a four-year-old mare for a Schofield pistol and twenty dollars. That mare stood over twelve hands high. I knew who they were, but I didn't care."

L.C. plucked up courage to ask if there was such a thing as the bogey-man—a big black man hiding in the woods. Grandpa replied, "Back in my day, folks used to say there was, just to scare ya." *Don't judge*

L.C.'s father sighed. "No, Junior, there's no bogey-man. Just a poor black fellow from Mississippi living in a shack by the river, hoping to be let alone—name is Sam. But if you mention him to anyone, I'll have to whup you."

Sheriff Lem knew all about the man, said to be wanted by the law in Mississippi. He still had a wife over there, a Kickapoo squaw he visited every so often when he picked up his mail. Those Mississippi lawmen said that Sam killed a couple of Cajuns, but as Sheriff Lem put it, "they prob'ly needed killing."

Grandpa glared at Lem, who burst out, "Well Hell, Dad, it ain't like Sam done anything over here!" At this point, L.C. slipped quietly off to bed—he'd have to wait for another day to ask what a "hoor" was.

Chapter 4

Depression-Era Treachery

E aster Sunday dawned as spring reached the height of an early bloom. Preacher Burton was set to minister at a Brush Arbor down on the White River; baptisms were deemed likely. Preacher Burton, a farmer by trade, wore overalls and traveled on horseback between Possum Waller and Pleasant Grove, trading off Sundays between the two Baptist churches. At Eastertime, he always came to the river. An unspoken agreement between the dry-landers and River People made the holiest day of the calendar an annual picnic and fish fry, crowned by a rather competitive Easter egg hunt. The twin communities brought together fresh catfish and barbecue—pulled pork and beef brisket—and the resultant feast was something to behold, especially in Arkansas of 1930. The country, still reeling from the crash of the previous October, now found the Depression beginning to seep into everyday life.

The families of St. Charles and surrounding areas gathered hopefully on the banks of the White River that Easter as they had for ages, singing the old songs, welcoming the season and its fresh crop of young lovers, married couples and newborn babes. The River People's tradition of taking in "woods colts" (the results of unintended pregnancies) ensured that every child born on the White River had a surname and a family. Adoption

When John Black and Helen Spence arrived at the Brush Arbor, heads turned. Helen, a vision in white, smiled and greeted folks, while John, carrying a stringer of catfish, nodded his customary silent hello. Making his way to a tree near the picnic tent, he nailed the catfish to the trunk, heads first. Gripping a pair of pliers, he handily stripped them one by one of their damp skins and filleted the pale flesh with his knife. *These might be th best days*

The Easter service and picnic—unremarkable save for the total contentment of those present—would be recalled wistfully over that year and the next, unlike the exact words of Preacher Burton's sermon. The frogs sang their goodnight chorus to sleepy, well-fed families returning to farmhouse or town, houseboat and river. Not one among the dry-landers or River People who gathered together that day had an inkling of the lengthy separation about to ensue. *Storms will come. BUT, JESUS!*

St. Charles boasted few streets, but streets and waterfront grew busy as summer unfolded. Men gathered in groups marked by clouds of tobacco smoke, intent on discussing the day's headlines and the week's gossip. Women met in the aisles of the Mercantile or beside the garden gate to converse in low voices, casting nervous glances toward children nearby. The youngsters caught the filtered tones of fear couched in repeated phrase and gesture but dared not question the grown-ups, the suddenly restless parents with worried faces and bewildered eyes that no longer met across the kitchen table. *Children pick up on fear*

"Depression? Why, there's always a depression in Arkansas. Who can tell the difference?" *complaining contaminates*

"The heat's bad this year—my hens quit laying."

"Never seen a dry spell like this so early. If it don't rain soon…" *Trust God.*

The voices trailed off. Rain, or rather the lack, was a main topic of conversation, punctuated by retellings of the latest financial uproar or big-city crime spree. According to general consensus, a nationwide breakout of lawlessness loomed, and the droughty weather merely augured the downfall. Arkansas, once a thruway for the James and Younger Gangs, had not shed its reputation as an outlaw hideout. During the Roaring Twenties, Arkansas' spa city of Hot Springs gained notoriety as a "wide open" haven for gangsters like Al Capone and Lucky Luciano. The bathhouse district there drew trainloads of tourists who arrived to take the waters, while the Southern Club's casino goings-on were an open secret—a secret that formed the reelection platform of Hot Springs mayor Leo McLaughlin.

The year 1930 witnessed the birth pangs of the Ma Barker Gang, as Fred *the old* Barker met Alvin "Creepy" Karpis when both were serving time in a Kansas prison. Clyde Barrow was about to get introduced to Bonnie Parker in some *Mary + Brad* steamy Texas dive. These and other renegades began making inexorable movements down various paths, all of which led into Arkansas, but their crimes and accompanying headlines were yet to come to a national stage.

During June, July and August, the weather alone held sway over the Delta, and all the news was bad.

"It's too hot," Helen moaned upon waking to another stifling day. Sitting up in bed, she brushed aside the mosquito netting, grumbling. "I'm goin' for a swim."

Cicero had already left to check the trotlines. Ada was stirring in the next room, her ever-present hand-rolled cigarette dangling perilously over the coffee cups. "You ain't just a-wolfin'," Ada remarked. "Mm-mm, child, you ain't just a-whistlin' Dixie!" Her chirping laughter followed. Helen tried to convince her stepmother to take a swim, and not for the first time. It was always the same: Ada was scared of the water. Years before, someone had picked her up and thrown her into the White River in a misguided attempt at a joke. She never got over it. Even when Edie, who could only watch as others swam, chimed in with words of encouragement, Ada adamantly refused. She was not going in, no matter if it was "a hunnerd degrees at daybreak."

But the only sure cure for the relentless heat was a cool plunge, and Helen took it as the sun cleared the trees. A thick layer of mist disappeared in shreds as she broke the water's sparkling surface. Countless blue-streaked minnows and striped fingerlings scattered, regrouping to surround the girl as she swam. Helen surfaced, blowing and kicking noisily to satisfy Ada, who had helped Edie to the deck chair and stood looking out over the water, nodding in approval. Ada feared snakes, too, and decreed that raising a racket was the best repellent for moccasins. Gliding through the current with steady strokes, Helen reached the houseboat ladder and scrambled up.

"Get some clothes on, and I'll make biscuits," Ada called. "There's still some peach preserves left."

The three women spent the sweltering morning doing as little as possible. Summer's hellish drought and record-breaking heat wave were causing calamities up and down the White River. There was talk of closing a stretch to barge traffic due to low levels. But the worst of it was being felt on land, where farmers watched helplessly as acres of corn and cotton shriveled. Gardens dried up; even the sorghum was wilting. Only tiny plots of kitchen herbs stayed stubbornly green. The land lay prone under a searing sky, whole fields yellowing and turning brown like leaves on a dying tree.

"I haven't seen it this bad since the war," Ada observed, spreading the last of 1929's peach preserves on a biscuit. Helen and Edie, knowing better than to inquire about the war, asked if she thought it would rain soon. "It'll come a hard rain, if it comes at all," was the stern reply.

Cicero returned around lunchtime. Stripping to his undershorts, he waded into the shallows with a cake of lye soap to take a leisurely bath. Helen brought over a clean flour sack, and he dried off and came aboard the houseboat.

"I was up by the mussel beds," he announced as Ada set out plates of fried catfish and cornbread. "The water's down so low—never seen the like—and the heat's so bad the damn mussels are burstin' open. Muckets and fantails spread out in the mud, a-poppin' like firecrackers."

"It's good for the divers, then," Ada said hopefully. "They can just grab 'em by the handful—won't even have to get their feet wet."

"Have to fight off the wild hogs first," Cicero replied with a bitter laugh. "Maybe they'll find a pearl." Arkansas' fierce breed of feral swine—the native "razorbacks"—favored the taste of mussel flesh and were known to crack open the shells with their powerful jaws when they could get to 'em. The sun was doing the hard part now. Having finished his meal, Cicero walked up the stage plank toward the tree line to have a smoke. He motioned for Helen to follow.

"The heat is gettin' to folks," her father began as the two stood in the shade. "I want you to keep your eyes and your wits about you—especially on the river. Don't go off by yourself, understand?"

Helen listened as he described the situation—he didn't want Ada or Edie to hear and fret, but things were worsening and not just in the Delta. It was all over the newspapers. Out west, on the big thousand-acre California farms where the drought wasn't even happening, crops were being allowed to rot in the fields. Cicero called it "the sin of the profiteers." He'd heard from Buck Joiner that the tenant farmers were having a time just feeding their kids. A sickness called pellagra was spreading like fire. It wasn't contagious like measles, but it was hitting the sharecroppers hard and tearing 'em down fast. It had something to do with the lack of fresh vegetables.

"A person can starve for a long time," Cicero muttered. When Helen asked if he'd seen Sheriff Lem lately, he quickly allayed her fears: "Your little buddy L.C. ain't gonna starve. The Browns are doin' just fine. Lem dressed out a deer t'other day." Warning again to "watch out for strangers on the river," Cicero left to take his catch to the icehouse.

When the River People disagreed or disputed with one another, the solution was often as simple as untying the houseboat from the bank, pulling up anchor and floating downstream away from the offending person or family. Feuds were settled quickly, with knives or guns and "an eye for an eye," what the locals called River Justice. Disputes over prime fishing holes, whiskey stills and territories claimed by hunter or moonshiner could turn deadly in an instant. Because the River People asked few questions, from time to time nameless and rootless men arrived to hide out in the impenetrable tangle of forest and swamp. Along the White, from Des Arc to Clarendon on down, miles of houseboat communities sheltered the occasional outlaw who was let be as long as no one got hurt. The summer of 1930 saw an influx of transients on the river as hungry men ranged across the country in search of something better than the nothing they had.

Night fell and the heat abated somewhat. Helen, sitting on deck slapping mosquitoes, spied a light bobbing toward the Spence houseboat—it was John Black, poling upriver in a flat-bottomed shell boat. He was come to show off his new carbide cap. John asked if Helen wanted to go frog-gigging. Cicero made certain John had his gun on him and grudgingly relented. The two embarked, Helen waving from her seat as John poled away. Cicero stood watching long after they disappeared around a bend, his pipe smoke hanging in the humid air.

"I got me a new snap-gig," John bragged, turning the skiff into the sluggish current. "My cousin traded a man some deer jerky for that and the carbide." He fiddled with the light on his cap, sending its little beam flickering through the darkness as they drifted downstream.

"Bet he traded some white lightning too," intoned Helen. Ignoring her comment, John turned his attention to avoiding stobs exposed by the low water. Lightning bugs flashed yellow among the trees. Frogs and cicadas hummed monotonously in the heavy air as the moon's crescent appeared from a cloud.

"Watch out for that limb," Helen cautioned as John ducked. "Snakes."

"That reminds me," John mused. "You ever see a frog rain? I did once, with my uncle up toward DeValls Bluff. It was about this time o'year. We were coming back from a mussel-shelling trip, and right as we got to the houseboat, it just opened up. The air was dark green and thick with frogs. They were hittin' us like rocks. It was all we could do to tie up the boat and get inside."

"Funny thing is," John continued, "Next morning, I went up to the levee to see the piles o'dead frogs. But there was nothing—not a single frog! I guess the critters cleaned 'em up in the middle of the night."

Helen asked if he would show her his trick of skinning the frog's legs like rolling down a pair of britches, but John shushed her. The frogs fell silent. Slowing the boat, he cut the light and listened. A call like a whippoorwill came from the blackness of the opposite bank. Seconds later, a whistle answered farther downstream. A speck of orange light glowed off in the woods—a distant pipe or cigarette. Helen grabbed an oar and joined John in turning the boat as the pair quickly paddled back the way they had come, careful not to utter a sound.

Independence Day was a bust: too dry for fireworks. The local boys left off their usual horse races because of the heat. Most weekends during summer—especially around the Fourth of July—were taken up with horse racing. The little crossroads community of Ethel, home to L.C.'s family, marked the site of a proud racing tradition. Young men from miles around gathered outside Ethel near a huge cypress tree—the biggest tree in Arkansas. Too big for any saw-blade, it had been spared the axe, and the road to Ethel was constructed around it. The riders raced the mile or so from the cypress to Ethel's general store, where the winner got a bottle of cold Coca-Cola and the crowd collected their bets.

Other summertime traditions went by the wayside. The Italian family next to the Dupslaffs made delicious "gelatty," as the kids called it. This summer, the cream wouldn't freeze. Poor Miz Dupslaff couldn't make wine; the blackberries baked on the vines. Saturday night barn dances fell off. It was too hot to move, much less dance.

The rising temperatures, like a fever refusing to break, fed into August as the very air turned sour and poisonous. Livestock ponds choked with rotting fish suffocated by the scummy water. Brush fires popped up continually; a haze shrouded the sky. The people began to mumble and whisper the nightmare words: typhoid, cholera. Prayers went up as famine spread. Fear of hunger spread, too. A horror and a denial of hunger gripped the plantation owners, along with a burning question: if the tenant farmers were given free food, would they become too "comfortable" to work? Politicians and big landowners met at the state capital in Little Rock to discuss the situation—over lunch, as was customary. The men succeeded in convincing one another that all was well. Governor Harvey Parnell saw no need for hunger relief. Neither did President Herbert Hoover, despite the drought having spread to nearly two dozen states. Free boxes of seed and accompanying pamphlets were prepared for distribution instead. An official statement was ascribed in recognition of "minimal actual suffering." Ada called it "the time of turnips and tears." Gov't manipulation

Helen grew tired of watching her world shrink. More than anything else, the heat was a confining thing, an obstacle to enjoying life on the river—except, of course, swimming, which River People did almost every day. Luckily, the cold-water spring's constant fountain never faltered. Its icy crystalline waters were a reminder that the dry spell could not last forever.

51

When autumn finally arrived to break the heat, it was too late for any hopes of harvest. Farmers complained impotently of the five-cent cotton and worthless seed corn. The River People were still able to feed themselves, however, and hunting and fishing guides still made money—along with the moonshiners, busy as ever. *people always numb*

One morning in December, Helen woke to the sound of voices outside her window. It was Cicero talking to a man about a fishing trip. "All right, Jack," she heard her father say, and then came sounds of boots scraping about on deck and the boat motor cranking up. Helen hurried to dress and went into the kitchen, where Ada sat staring at the fire.

"Bundle up, child," her stepmother sighed. "Your father forgot to take the food I made. We're gonna row it out to him." When Helen asked about Edie, Ada replied, still gazing into the iron stove, "We'll be back before she wakes up."

As the two women paddled away from the houseboat, Helen drank in deep draughts of frosty air. The river was running low, and they made good time, heading to a fishing hole upstream. Helen wondered aloud who "Jack" could be, but before Ada could reply, voices ahead sounded, raised in anger. Cicero's boat came into view. The two men were standing in the boat arguing. The women watched as Cicero lost his balance and swayed toward the other man. The man's arm went out; there came a loud report, and Cicero sank to his knees. Ada grabbed Helen by the arm and squeezed hard, but Helen was too stunned to scream. The man looked over his shoulder and saw them. He motioned with the gun for them to come closer.

"He wouldn't show me where the still money is," the man said with a frown, slurring his words. He looked young. As Helen and Ada watched in terror, he shoved Cicero's body into the water as though it were a floating log. Suddenly, Ada stood up in the boat and addressed the man: "I'll show ya. This here girl's simple-minded. She don't know where the money's hid." *drunk*

The man called Jack reached over and hauled Ada into the boat. Grabbing the oars from Helen, he pushed her boat away with his foot and turned to crank the motor. As Helen drifted downstream, paralyzed with fear, the two continued into the distance until the boat's wake disappeared. Hours later, when some fishermen found her, the girl was still in shock.

Steamboat on the White River at St. Charles, Arkansas, circa 1920s. *Courtesy of L.C. Brown.*

Depression-era watercolor study of a White River houseboat by Laura Flint, wife of the commanding officer of the Civilian Conservation Corps' (CCC) "floating camp" at St. Charles, possibly circa 1935. *Courtesy of Dale Woodiel.*

Opposite, top: St. Charles's icehouse on the bluff overlooking the White River, circa 1920s. *Courtesy of L.C. Brown.*

Opposite, bottom: Ferry at St. Charles, circa 1920. *Courtesy of L.C. Brown.*

Helen Spence and Buster Eaton, possibly circa 1928. Married briefly, the two separated when Helen returned to the Spence family houseboat at St. Charles. *Courtesy of L.C. Brown.*

Helen Spence and Buster Eaton at St. Charles, posed atop a contraption once used to weigh cotton bales for loading onto paddle-wheelers. *Courtesy of L.C. Brown.*

Above: A young L.C. Brown with "Bill," his pet goat, possibly circa 1928. *Courtesy of L.C. Brown.*

Right: The Brown family, circa 1920: Lem, Estella and L.C.'s big brother, John Homer. *Courtesy of L.C. Brown.*

Arkansas County sheriff Lemuel Cressie Brown Sr., with his one-eyed horse, "Ol' Good-Eye," possibly circa 1918. *Courtesy of L.C. Brown.*

L.C. Brown. When this photo was taken, L.C. was already "running traps" and hunting fox squirrels, possibly circa 1930. *Courtesy of L.C. Brown.*

L.C.'s grandparents, Homer and Nora Brown, at home on the Brown family farm in Ethel, Arkansas, 1930. *Courtesy of L.C. Brown.*

L.C. Brown joined the army at age seventeen, becoming a paratrooper and sniper for the Pathfinders during World War II. *Courtesy of L.C. Brown.*

Cargo chute at Crockett's Bluff near St. Charles showing bags of rice being stacked on board a barge below the Prange family warehouse, possibly circa 1920. *Courtesy of Dale Woodiel.*

Houseboat on the White River near Crockett's Bluff (several miles north of St. Charles), possibly circa 1920. Crockett's Bluff is named for Captain Robert Crockett, grandson of folk hero Davy Crockett. *Courtesy of Dale Woodiel.*

GIRL SLAYER, FREED, PLANS NEW 'START'

Right: John Black's collection of newspaper clippings about Helen Spence. *Courtesy of L.C. Brown.*

Below: Steamboat on the White River at DeValls Bluff, circa 1910. *Courtesy of the archives of the Butler Center for Arkansas Studies, Central Arkansas Library System.*

Above: The church beside the cemetery at St. Charles no longer exists; this photograph was taken in the early years of the twentieth century. *Courtesy of L.C. Brown.*

Left: Detail of photo showing Helen (standing) and her sister, Edna ("Edie") Spence, posed with a quilt as backdrop, possibly circa 1916. *Courtesy of the Lower White River Museum State Park, Des Arc, Arkansas.*

Above: The Great Flood
of 1927 caused the White
River to flow backward
as the Mississippi
River's catastrophic rise
inundated the Delta. This
view of DeValls Bluff
shows the extent of the
flooding. *Courtesy of the
Lower White River Museum
State Park, Des Arc, Arkansas.*

Right: Mussel-shelling was
once a major industry
in eastern Arkansas,
with several area button
factories manufacturing
native mother-of-pearl
buttons. The entire
industry collapsed due
to the post–World War
II rise of cheap plastic
combined with the
effects of Bull Shoals
Dam and dredging by
the U.S. Army Corps
of Engineers. Mussels
yielded rare pearls; the
oblong ones were called
"River Tears." *Courtesy of
L.C. Brown.*

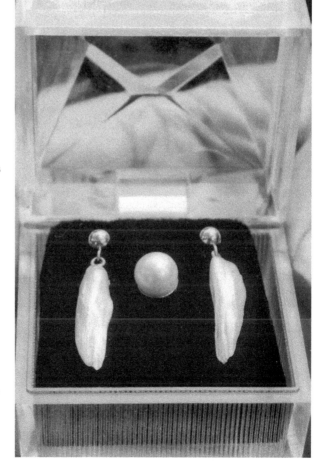

Boat-building by the Civilian Conservation Corps at the St. Charles CCC "floating camp," 1935. *Courtesy of the Collections of the Arkansas History Commission.*

The CCC "floating camp" on the White River at St. Charles, 1935. FDR's New Deal put Arkansans to work even as the government takeover of the White River bottomlands spelled the beginning of the end of the River People's way of life. *Courtesy of the Collections of the Arkansas History Commission.*

Above: Steamboats docked on the White River at Des Arc, 1910. *Courtesy of the archives of the Butler Center for Arkansas Studies and the Central Arkansas Library System.*

Right: Expanded view of Cicero and Helen Spence and John Black, as well as unidentified boys and hunter, at a fur trading barn in St. Charles, possibly circa 1918. *Courtesy of L.C. Brown.*

The author's family houseboat situated on the banks of the White River near Clarendon, Arkansas, possibly circa 1950. (Note the faux brick siding.) *Courtesy of Matt White.*

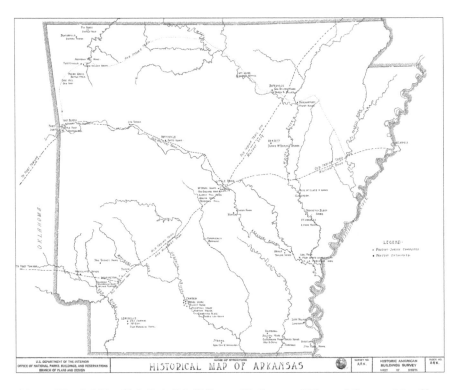

Arkansas Historical Map, Little Rock, Pulaski County, AR. Courtesy of Library of Congress, Prints & Photographs Division, HABS [or HAER or HALS], HABS ILL, 16-CHIG, 33-2.

Sharecropper with homemade water wagon, Arkansas, October 1935. *Courtesy of Ben Shaun, Library of Congress, Prints & Photographs Division, FSA/OWI Collection, LC-USF3301-006068-M1 DLC.*

Brush Arbor on the White River, Arkansas County, circa 1900, by Dayton Bowers. *Courtesy of LC Brown and the Anna Grace Bowers Brown Manuscript Collection, Butler Center for Arkansas Studies.*

Sand Mills (vicinity), Arkansas. Men of the 354 Engineer Regiment, U.S. Army Signal Corps, at work on the levee on the White River, May 1943. *Courtesy of Library of Congress, Prints & Photographs Division, FSA/OWI Collection, LC-USW33-029183-C DLC.*

Baptism, Arkansas County, circa 1900, by Dayton Bowers. *Courtesy of LC Brown and the Anna Grace Bowers Brown Manuscript Collection, Butler Center for Arkansas Studies.*

Dust storm approaching Stratford, Texas. Dust bowl surveying in Texas, April 18, 1935.
Courtesy of NOAA, George E. Marsh Album, Historic C&GS Collection.

Families of evicted sharecroppers on the Dibble plantation, Parkin (vicinity), Arkansas.
*Courtesy of John Vachon, January 1936, Library of Congress, Prints & Photographs Division, FSA/
OWI Collection, LC-USF34-014005-E DLC.*

Three ladies on a bluff overlooking the White River, Arkansas County, circa 1900, by Dayton Bowers. *Courtesy of LC Brown and the Anna Grace Bowers Brown Manuscript Collection, Butler Center for Arkansas Studies.*

Young girl thought to be Helen Spence around age 10, circa 1922, at grave decorated with mussel shells and yancopin flowers, Arkansas County, by Dayton Bowers. *Courtesy of LC Brown and the Anna Grace Bowers Brown Manuscript Collection, Butler Center for Arkansas Studies.*

Bull Shoals Dam, constructed on the upper White River, changed everything downstream. Bull Shoals Dam construction (1948) picture collection, number 3250. *Courtesy of Special Collections, University of Arkansas Libraries, Fayetteville, Arkansas.*

Civilian Conservation Corps worker and cypress tree near St. Charles, circa 1935. *Courtesy of Archives of the U.S. Fish and Wildlife Service, White River National Wildlife Refuge, St. Charles, Arkansas.*

The *Mary Woods* steamboat, docked near Crockett's Bluff on the lower White River, possibly circa 1920. *Courtesy of Dale Woodiel.*

Chapter 5
"She Showed No Remorse"

N ews of Cicero Spence's murder raced up and down the White River. The River People shook their heads at such a betrayal of hospitality, voices dropping to compare notes on what happened to poor Ada. The young man named Jack—Jack Worls—had flown into a rage upon finding no buried coins, no wad of bills stuffed inside a mason jar hidden in some tree hollow. Unleashing the full measure of his wrath, he beat Ada nearly to death. The citizens of Arkansas County found themselves whispering about a subject rarely discussed: rape. Jack Worls was quickly apprehended, and in the days that followed, Sheriff Lem consulted at length with Uncle Archie and Grandpa Homer, voicing amazement that "this no-good" was actually going to stand trial in DeWitt. It puzzled Sheriff Lem that the River People didn't "just handle it themselves."

Ada languished in the Memphis hospital for weeks, while Helen and Edie kept a bedside vigil. When Ada began to slip away, a pair of distant cousins arrived by train all the way from Chickasaw, Oklahoma. They came to "fetch Miss Edie to Chickasee," explaining to Helen as kindly as they could that there was no future for a cripple on the river. Edie would have a proper home in Oklahoma. The sisters made their goodbyes, and Helen prepared to return to St. Charles an orphan. Ada succumbed to her wounds on January 7, 1931.

A few days before, an event took place that propelled Arkansas' desperate farm families to the national spotlight. Drought, ruination and widespread hunger, combined with Governor Parnell's insistence that "conditions" were "not alarming," all came to a head in the town of England, Arkansas—a place known as the state's breadbasket. The floodplain of the Arkansas River stretches hundreds of miles northwest of St. Charles. Settlers and timber men long ago cleared the virgin forest of giant oak and red gum. Arkansas' "Grand Prairie" began to grow plantations. Season after season, tenant farmers walked behind mules, plowing ever-longer furrows. A fenced, flattened and straightened desert of cotton and corn, England's former glory was stricken. The once-fertile land gave up a harvest of dust.

A Red Cross office was hastily assembled in England just in time for Christmas. Moved by the plight of a local widow's hungry brood, sharecroppers and tenant farmers began gathering in downtown England on January 3, 1931. Hundreds of people (some armed) overflowed the small office, loudly demanding the help promised by the American Red Cross. But the staff lacked even the necessary printed forms. No applications for aid were available, and there was no stock of food on hand.

The desperate crowd appealed to England's merchants for relief. After receiving assurances of repayment from the Red Cross, the storekeepers opened their doors to the mob and tragedy was averted without violence. However, a reporter with ties to the Associated Press happened to be on hand, and soon the story of England's "food riot" ricocheted across the front pages of newspapers coast to coast. This dubious distinction—the first food riot of the Great Depression but certainly not the last—proved embarrassing for Arkansas politicians, and some began to move, however belatedly, to address the problem.

As the trial date for Jack Worls approached, L.C. Brown grew excited at the prospect of accompanying his father to the DeWitt Courthouse. Having shed tears over the Spence family tragedy, L.C. just wanted to see Helen again. It was some comfort to hear that she was safe and staying in DeWitt with Sheriff McAllister's family; the boy was also cheered to know John Black had taken in Cicero's hound dog. But sometimes, lying in bed at night, it was hard not to picture the old gray-planked houseboat rocking in the current, windows dark and vacant in the mist.

Mid-January brought a rare snowstorm. To the delight of L.C. and his cousins, their neighbor, George Williams, hitched the tall draft horses to the sleigh, and everyone piled in for the ride from Ethel to St. Charles. Heavy gray clouds lowered the sky, and more thick flakes fell along the way. By the time the party reached Main Street, entire families were playing in the drifts. The sleigh full of noisy children passed through downtown as people cheered from sidewalks, yards and porches. At a street corner marked by a spreading tree, a cloaked figure stood apart from the rest, hands tucked inside a snow-white rabbit-fur muff. It was Helen! The boy waved, his urgent cries overwhelmed by the cousins' laughter. When the horses took a second turn through the streets, the girl was gone. L.C. did not know it then, but this was to be the last time he saw Helen Spence.

"Wake up, Junior—we got to get on the road," Sheriff Lem said a few mornings later. The day of the trial had finally come. Mother and Grandma Nora tearfully excused themselves from the spectacle, remaining behind while the Brown family men set off for the courthouse. Melting snow dotted the fields, and the breeze carried a scent of cedar, hinting at false spring. As Sheriff Lem reached DeWitt's crowded town square, he sternly reminded L.C. to play outside on the courthouse lawn. Children were not allowed in the courtroom. L.C. jumped from the car to join the throng. It seemed all of Arkansas County was milling about the grand old building. The boy was soon absorbed in a rather muddy game of kickball and did not notice when Helen stepped from a car and, surrounded by deputies, ascended the courthouse steps.

Sometime later, as the children were commencing snap-the-whip, a volley of gunshots sounded from inside the building. The kids froze in place. Some older boys began yelling, "Shoot out! Shoot out!" as groups of girls burst into eerie wails. One by one, the first-floor windows of the courthouse slid up with a bang, and men and women began tumbling out. They thrashed in the hedges, scrambling away from the pandemonium. Sounds of furniture crashing and high-pitched shrieks erupted in the interior. L.C. moved toward the entrance and almost got knocked down by a rush of folks streaming out the door in panic. The boy went to stand with a group of Pleasant Grove kids—they took turns casting furtive glances to see if Sheriff Lem's son would cry. After an eternity, Grandpa Homer emerged alongside L.C.'s big brother. Finally, Sheriff Lem came down the steps. "Get in the car, Junior," his father said in a choked voice.

The ride home was grim. Sheriff Lem eventually described the scene: for hours, Helen sat quietly in the front row of the gallery listening to the testimony, her expression a blank. She wore the same red velvet suit and rabbit-fur muff as at the Reunion dance. The judge told Jack Worls to stand while the jury received some instructions—it looked like a solid case. "But then, you never know," Lem muttered.

The *New York Times* picked up the story, blurting on its front page on January 20, 1931 ("Girl Kills Alleged Slayer of Father in Court; Fires as Arkansas Jury Is About to Get Case"):

Drawing a pistol as the jury rose to decide the fate of the man on trial, Mrs. Ruth Spence Eaton, 18, shot and killed Jack Worls...the only statement the girl would make after the shooting was: "He killed my daddy." She showed no remorse.

The AP newsman who scooped the England Food Riot had been joined by others of his ilk. Adventuresome journalists were hunkered below the Mason-Dixon line, all set to write about Arkansas, the degraded epicenter of the Great Depression. But this breaking story was something else. Gripping copy, a sympathetic heroine and none of the politics of starvation—it would practically write itself. Despite the use of Helen's defunct married name and the question of whether she was younger than eighteen at the time, the *New York Times*' account is fairly accurate—accuracy becoming a rarity in subsequent stories about Helen. One reporter promptly dubbed her "The Swamp Angel."

After plugging Jack Worls four times in the chest, the girl dropped her arm and stood waiting for the ensuing chaos. Sheriff Lem, clutching his pipe with a shaky hand, was the first to approach. He tapped Helen on the shoulder, and she wheeled around, lifting a pearl-handled lady's pistol formerly concealed inside the rabbit-fur muff.

"Sheriff Lem," she cried, "I thought you were Big Boy Boydstone!" Constable Boydstone smoked a similar pipe as Lem and was about the same height. Apparently, "Big Boy" had insulted Helen's virtue during a pretrial interview.

"I came right near shooting you!" the girl gasped, handing over the gun. She followed several deputies down a hallway and into a side room, Sheriff Lem in tow. Once inside, Lem tried to pry open the chamber and empty the remaining bullets, but his hands kept shaking. "Let me help you—it tends to stick," Helen said, snatching the pistol. Every man in the room dove under the nearest piece of furniture; Helen deftly removed the bullets and placed them on a table. Lem summed up the entire episode: "All Hell broke loose today."

From this point on, John Black, along with everyone else on the river, began seeking out newspaper articles, editorials, anything and everything printed about Helen. Editors agreed that Helen Spence was great copy. From Memphis's *Commercial Appeal* to the *Pine Bluff Commercial*, the *DeWitt Era-Enterprise*, the *Arkansas Democrat* and the *Arkansas Gazette* (known as the "Old Gray Lady"), some dailies had morning and afternoon editions. The *Gazette*'s January 20 front page featured two contradictory accounts of the courtroom shooting, headlined in all caps: "GIRL, 17, AVENGES DEATH OF FATHER," went one, while the second read, "FEARED ACQUITTAL OF FATHER'S

Killer." In those days of absent bylines, there was no way of knowing who wrote the stories. The *Gazette*'s dueling accounts reported variously that Helen had dropped the gun under a bench as well as that she handed the weapon over to a deputy, as per Sheriff Lem's account. The River People objected to the newspaper's claim that Helen shot Jack Worls in the back—a detail disputed by witnesses. People read and reread the *Gazette*'s litany of unfounded accusations and sheer gossip concerning the Spence family. All of Arkansas County was abuzz.

Several topics covered by the *Gazette* that day were enough to ensure heated debate up and down the river as to the veracity of the report and the reliability of newspapers in general. For one thing, the *Gazette* published the name of a man who claimed to have been on the boat with Jack Worls and Cicero Spence—the man's name is spelled both "Nipson" and "Nitson" throughout the article—but he had turned state's evidence and testified that Worls acted in self-defense. The River People called this collusion. Ada's death meant that the state lost its principal witness; the fact that Helen was not called to testify indicates that she was indeed under the age of eighteen and would not have been considered reliable by the court.

Moreover, the *Gazette* referred to Cicero Spence as having himself been convicted of murdering a man on the river, a charge he was obviously unable to defend. (The *Gazette* withdrew this charge in subsequent published accounts.) But the most damning slur, according to those who knew the Spence family, came in a paragraph that described a supposed recent suicide attempt by Helen that left her "seriously wounded." Without quotes from hospital officials, the vague report simply stated, "At the time she attempted to end her life she said that she was despondent because she had been out of work and had been unable to find employment."

Perhaps the most accurate reportage of either *Gazette* article comes in a passage detailing Helen's characteristic, unrelenting spunk, a fearlessness shared by those brought up under the code of River Justice:

> She laughed telling of the flight of judge, jurors, lawyers and spectators from the court room when she opened fire....She hopes to obtain her freedom as she does not believe that she committed a crime. When the electric chair was mentioned, she laughed again.

Helen was famous now, or infamous, depending on who was doing the talking. She was released into the custody of the sheriff and his wife while her case was sent to the grand jury. Miss Mattie Roy, who ran a rooming house in DeWitt, went to visit the McAllisters. Like many folks, Miss Mattie was wrought up about the plight of the orphan girl. She offered to keep Helen at her boardinghouse while the case was being appealed. "If she leaves, I'll whip her," Miss Mattie promised, reminding the sheriff that "a good spanking would help anything." Miss Mattie was thanked for her kind offer but told no. She left in a huff.

Helen faced a charge of first-degree murder, according to the *Gazette*'s report of January 22, 1931 ("Seventeen-Year-Old Courtroom Slayer Indicted by Grand Jury"). An article published that same day adds a disturbing coda to Arkansas' ongoing drought-related disaster:

> *POVERTY-STRICKEN FARMER ENDS LIFE*
> *Slashes Throat With Razor When Cows and Hogs Are Taken Away.*
>
> *Prescott, Jan. 21.—Despondent over crop failure and lack of food for his wife and five children, A.R. Sheltz, 47, farmer living one mile north of Boughton, committed suicide in the road near his home by cutting his throat with a razor this morning... His landlord, to whom he was indebted, yesterday took his cow and hogs as part of payment.*

Meanwhile, Helen took a job at the Rothenhoffer Café in DeWitt. She proved an efficient waitress, and customers began coming from miles around just to catch a glimpse of Arkansas County's notorious "Gun Girl." The café was run by a Greek man named Jim Bohots, a man with a reputation for manhandling his female employees. Jim Bohots was about to come face to face with the code of the White River and Helen Ruth Spence.

Chapter 6

A Chance at Liberty

As the spring of 1931 approached, Helen remained in the DeWitt home of the local sheriff. The girl was careful to express gratitude at every turn, but life among the dry-landers was nothing like the White River. The littlest thing brought a pang: a balmy breeze through the window, or the guestroom's chenille bedspread that called to mind Ada's quilts. City food was too rich and lacked savor; missing was the plainer joy of fresh-caught fish fried in cornmeal. Harbinger wildflowers appeared all over town, carpets of white and pink spring beauties, but Helen no longer went barefoot.

As the case of *Arkansas v. Spence* wound its halting way through the system of appeal and delay, the girl adopted a routine of waking, working and returning home. Church on Sundays was followed by afternoons indoors, the stillness broken by the ticking of the clock. When not waitressing at the café, Helen sat at a desk in her room and wrote lengthy letters to Edie. Sometimes in the sun parlor, attempting to sew or crochet, her hands stilled as she drifted into daydreams. The sunset curfew imposed by Judge Waggoner grew irksome as the days lengthened.

The Rothenhoffer Café sits like a brick box in downtown DeWitt, not far from courthouse square. The two-story building features a wide bank of sinuous glass blocks windowing the front of the ground floor. The upstairs level is divided into a few small apartments. Mrs. Rothenhoffer lived upstairs; so did one of the waitresses, Ina Mayberry, who took a liking to Helen and soon invited her to join her as a roommate. Yet Helen needed to bide her time and work hard. Things were tough all over; it was no use complaining.

February's clear, frigid nights closed with a flourish as the last full moon of winter rose. Some ancient tribes call this the "Hunger Moon" due to the month's harsh hunting conditions. From the oracles of newspapers came word that the old name still held true: dark days of Depression and want were spelled out in black-and-white. On March 2, 1931, the Associated Press reported on a federal inquiry that found "an alarming tendency toward monopolistic control of the food of the nation by a small group of powerful corporations." Protests by starving sharecroppers were spreading. McCrory, an Arkansas Delta town, was the scene of the latest "demonstration." The *Arkansas Gazette* published a harrowing account of a local farmer's widow (the item is buried on page twenty):

> *DERANGED MOTHER SLAYS HER CHILD*
> *Woman Suffering from Pellagra Slashes Eight-Year-Old Boy's Throat.*
> *Special to the Gazette.*
>
> *McCrory, March 2.—Mentally deranged as the result of several months [sic] illness from pellagra, Mrs. Lillie Chappell, widow, aged 45, who lives seven miles southeast of McCrory, slashed the throat of her youngest son, Woodrow, aged eight, with a razor early this morning, causing death. She was getting the children ready for school when she attacked the youngest.*
> *Mrs. Chappell declared she would rather see her son dead than to have him suffer from the dread disease. The woman was taken to the state Hospital for Nervous Diseases…The child will be buried tomorrow in the Odd Fellows cemetery here. He is survived by three brothers, two sisters and his mother.*

Despite a mounting record of epic disaster, America's business tycoons prided themselves on seeing beyond tales of actual suffering. The president of United States Steel Corporation took the opportunity to publicly declare his opinion that "the peak of the financial depression had been passed." In a speech to the 1931 convention of the National Canners and Wholesale Grocers Association, steel magnate James A. Farrell boasted of "a considerable increase" in the business of the steel industry, as well as "collateral and unrelated lines."

Helen, like any young person, was occupied with the business at hand. She had no time for the news or newsmen. Folks at the café's lunch counter tended to have a slice of pie, several cups of coffee and a smoke. Diners relaxed with newspaper in hand, perusing the medium of the day, deaf to the clatter and bustle of the restaurant. Helen got used to being pointed out by people waving from booths. The girl was popular; she made waitressing look easy and fun—a trick that never fails to attract attention from the boss, for good or ill.

The café manager, Jim Bohots, was called "the Greek" (out of earshot). His management skills comprised a mix of bullying and/or sweaty groping. It was only a matter of time before the Greek tried to manage Helen Spence.

At first, he seemed to see the good in her presence and indulged streams of admirers and well-wishers. But his sense of spite prevailed. When a muddy, buckskin-clad John Black came stomping into the café one raw spring day and asked for Helen, the Greek's patience ran out. He wasn't running a place for river rats, and he damn sure wasn't running a place for tramps and moonshiners! Bohots pushed through the swinging doors into the kitchen, slamming pots and pans, his curses overheard in the dining room. John turned on his heel and exited the building as Bohots retreated to the café's windowless office, presumably to uncork a bottle. Similar scenes were to be played out over the ensuing months as Helen maintained her humble position despite growing, unsought notoriety. It seemed that the closer she got to a pardon from the governor, the nearer she came to losing her job.

The girl's efforts impressed Judge W.J. Waggoner, however, and he gave permission for her to move in with Ina Mayberry above the café. A measure of freedom seemed possible within those four walls, situated where DeWitt's downtown streets merge like angular rivers. And Ina was the ideal roommate. Thoughtful and sweet-natured, she kept the tiny apartment neat as a pin and shared her meager belongings. In the mornings, she and Helen dressed hurriedly and rushed downstairs before sunrise to ready the restaurant— Bohots never showed up before eight o'clock.

The empty dining room was a welcome sight in the morning, silver coffee urns and ceramic dishes gleaming in the half-light. The girls worked quickly; soon came the aroma of coffee brewing and bacon sizzling, biscuits baking and doughnuts frying. Golden-brown "sinkers" were stacked in pyramids along the varnished counter, ready for the coffee drinkers. An island of simple routine, the café appeared a sort of home. The waitresses, arriving and departing their shifts, became a choreographed family—albeit a family in which Bohots played the role of brutish, drunken father.

One morning in midsummer, Helen opened the door to sweep the front sidewalk, and there stood John Black. The girls pulled him inside. Ina poured coffee while John regarded Helen.

"You're too thin," the young man declared. "Don't they feed you here?" Helen responded by peppering him with questions. He was in town for supplies, afterward heading to the Black River, up north a ways. He was going to do some mussel-shelling with his uncle and wouldn't return to Arkansas County for a month, maybe two. "Depends on the weather," the youth said, reaching for a doughnut. The girls begged him to be careful up on the Black River.

"Don't y'all worry," John replied. "God don't want me and Hell's already full."

The companions were laughing at this old saw when the Greek burst through the front door, red-faced and sweating, and began barking orders. "What the hell you think this is? A soup kitchen?" Bohots roared at John's departing back.

Summer melted into fall, and Helen's fate remained unresolved. In November, the café buzzed with news of an unprecedented action by Governor Parnell. He had appointed a United States senator's widow named Hattie Caraway to finish out her late husband's term. A woman in the Senate—anything could happen! With the Depression deepening and 1932's election year looming, Parnell faced a tough campaign. After all, the governor still promoted self-help as the road to recovery even as his highway program bankrupted state coffers.

There is something spiteful in the short month of February that seeks to despoil the hopes of the New Year. February 1932, already bleak and dreary enough, got ugly fast. Jim Bohots had been on the rampage for days. His jealousy of the occasional reporter hanging around the café knew no bounds. It didn't matter that the newsmen were merely seeking updates on Helen's appeal to the state Supreme Court—every man was the Greek's rival. He'd ban 'em all from his place—he wasn't running no place for trash!

Then John Black came through town, sparking the usual scene complete with Bohots's threats of firing, even violence. This time, the Greek begged Helen to take a ride with him after work. They'd hash it all out. They just needed to talk. There was no privacy at the café. They would get some air, take a drive. He had a nice car. She would see he wasn't a bad man. Didn't she like her job? The Greek pleaded and sulked.

Next morning, as the girls were preparing to open the restaurant, two grim-faced officers appeared bearing bad news. Jim Bohots was dead, shot with his own gun. Helen was being taken in for questioning. She handed the broom to a stunned Ina, grabbed her coat and hat and left with the deputies.

Helen disavowed any knowledge of the Greek's comings and goings. The man had been discovered parked beside a large oak tree outside town, slumped behind the steering wheel of his car. The place was a well-known "trysting spot," and the officers went about their task without enthusiasm. Bohots had been the subject of universal dislike in DeWitt. When the case went cold and no charges were filed, the general consensus ran toward "he probably needed killing."

The wheels of commerce turn blindly, Depression or no, lifting or crushing at random those with a shoulder to the grindstone. As 1932's election year spectacle played out, life moved as in a dream. No longer a river girl yet not a dry-lander, Helen simply continued, a betwixt-and-between. The court's final decision remained a question mark hanging overhead, a constant invisible presence. The question was finally answered shortly before the gubernatorial election: Arkansas' Supreme Court overturned the judgment of five years that Helen faced for killing Jack Worls. Instead, she was allowed to plead guilty to manslaughter. She received a sentence of two years at the women's prison in Jacksonville, also known as "the Pea Farm."

From a history of slave labor, Arkansas' prison system had evolved in name only. The scandal of "convict leasing" was no more, yet prisoners still toiled in the fields. These same fields served as unmarked pauper's graves when forgotten prisoners fell from heat, overwork or other, unspecified causes. Helen began her sentence on October 11, 1932.

Harvey Parnell lost the election and retired from politics in disgrace, his most notable achievement being the appointment of Hattie Caraway. Senator Caraway—known as "Silent Hattie"—went on to win a landmark election to a full term and became a stalwart supporter of President Roosevelt's New Deal. Meanwhile, Arkansas' incoming Governor, Marion Futrell, parroted his predecessor concerning the scourge of poverty. Governor Futrell blamed sharecroppers and tenant farmers for their ills. He went so far as to say that the poor "were not worth the powder and lead it would take to blow out their brains."

Against this transitory backdrop, Helen's brief incarceration proved more refuge than punishment. The Depression was taking place outside prison walls, where despairing broken men drank carbolic acid or slashed themselves with razors. Bullets became the new mode of suicide as the wealthy lost everything except their gun collections.

Protected by ongoing appeals for parole and exalted to some degree by advance publicity, Helen did not have to work in the fields. She was locked inside a shabby, drafty dormitory among women not unlike herself—America's once-hopeful youth of the Great Depression. Her fellow inmates treated the girl like a little sister, and the days flowed into winter's mundane routine.

The state's prosecuting attorney, George Hartje, continued working to get Helen paroled. In a letter to the board of parole dated May 31, 1933, he answered the usual questions: Was the reputation of the applicant good or bad? (Good.) Was this the applicant's first offense? (Yes.) Were there any mitigating circumstances? To this question, Hartje responded, "The deceased [Jack Worls] had killed father and assaulted mother or stepmother—her act was one of revenge." In recommending parole for Helen, George F. Hartje concluded, "I…recommend that she be instructed not to return to Arkansas County to live—she was suspected of killing another man after the above killing for which she was sentenced, but upon investigation by the grand jury, I am thoroughly convinced she did not do it."

And so, a few days later, Helen left the Pea Farm a free woman, albeit an exile. She was under strict orders not to return to the only home she had ever known: DeWitt, nor St. Charles, where her elderly grandmother still lived. She was forbidden from going to her reclusive uncle, Pless Spence, who kept a houseboat on the White River. Helen's smiling face was splashed across the front page of the *Memphis Commercial Appeal* under the headline: "Girl Slayer, Freed, Plans New 'Start.' Helen Eaton Spence, Avenger of Father's Death, to Begin Life Again in Some Far Off Place."

Helen is quoted as saying, "I want to start all over again… I am going where no one knows me." And she did. For almost an entire week, she kicked around Little Rock and, using an assumed name, quickly secured a job as a waitress. At least, that's what the *Arkansas Gazette* reported, even going so far as to name the restaurant. However, Pea Farm records contradict the *Gazette*. A parole document and an employment document, both signed by Helen and a man named "W.B. Graham," indicate otherwise. W.B. Graham was the School Superintendent for neighboring Lonoke County during the 1930s; he paid $1,000 for Helen's parole bond, an amount equivalent to $14,000 today. The Arkansas Women's Prison's practice of debt peonage— or debt concubinage—cannot be ruled out, and may help explain what happened next: Then Helen did something no one saw coming. On June 15, 1933, the girl put on her nicest dress, walked into the Little Rock police station and openly confessed to the killing of Jim Bohots.

Chapter 7

Trapped in Hell

Helen's surprise confession came so closely on the heels of her release from prison that Memphis's *Commercial Appeal* simply reran the previous week's photograph. Headlined "Helen Eaton, Revenge Killer, Confesses to Second Murder," the lengthy article details how the "attractive, tastefully dressed young brunette calmly told of circumstances surrounding the killing."

Seeking out Little Rock police chief James Pitcock, the girl admitted that the death of her former boss had "preyed on her mind since it occurred." She described Jim Bohots's continual harassment at the café, his "unwelcome attentions" and his threat that if she did not "date" him, he would kill someone close to her. Helen refused to disclose this unnamed person's identity, so newsmen substituted the phrase "her sweetheart."

Helen had agreed to go for a drive on the night in question and talk things over, but to her chagrin, the Greek stopped the car outside DeWitt. The place he pulled over: the so-called trysting spot. The *Commercial Appeal* reported what happened next:

> *Her companion then started making overtures to her and "pawing over" her, she related. She attempted to get him out of the car by asking him to see if he would repair the motor trouble, but he remained in the automobile.*
>
> *When he declared he could not start the motor, and did not try, the young woman said she reached into a car pocket where she knew he kept a pistol, drew the weapon and fired one shot. The shot struck him in the chest, Bohots remaining upright on the seat but making no sound.*

Then the young woman opened the car door, and standing with one foot
on the running board, she fired two more shots.
"I thought he might not die," she explained.

Helen was now firmly ensnared by the system. It mattered not that
she had willingly come forward; her timing was off. Prosecuting Attorney
George Hartje had vouchsafed Helen's innocence; suddenly his official role
was reversed. Seldom does an instrument of the state admit a wrong, much
less an error in judgment. The story hit the afternoon papers on June 15,
1933; by July 3, Helen was back in Arkansas County facing Judge Waggoner
and an indictment for murder in the second degree. Waiving her right to
counsel, the girl put her fate in the hands of men she trusted, authorities
grown familiar to her over the past two years. The *Arkansas Gazette* (July 3,
1933, DeWitt) reported "10-YEAR SENTENCE FOR HELEN SPENCE: Confessed
Slayer of DeWitt Café Owner Returns to Women's Farm." The brief article
describes the girl's reaction to the sentence of ten years' hard labor:

> *Helen remained calm while Judge W.J. Waggoner sentenced her. She*
> *smiled as Judge Waggoner told her that he hoped she would "choose better*
> *associates" when she completed her sentence and "stay out of trouble."*

The court adjourned for the Independence Day holiday, and Helen
returned to the Pea Farm in Jacksonville with no hope of parole for three
and a half years. Back on the river, John Black read and reread his growing
collection of news clippings, carefully packing them away each time.

There was one benefit to the latest twist in the saga of Helen Spence, and
it fell squarely in the lap of Police Chief James Pitcock. Seizing on the story's
public relations potential as well as its visual appeal, the old lawman had
photographs made of the confession. Black-and-white pictures reveal Chief
Pitcock's rotund, cigar-chomping presence met by Helen's determined gaze
and casual air. Pitcock's white summer suit—linen or seersucker, by the cut of
it—contrasts Helen's polka-dot dress as they sit knee to knee and eye to eye.

The summer of 1933 brought renewed drought and heat—the Dust Bowl
of the Great Depression was in its nascent stages. Across the plains, "black
blizzards" came roaring from west to east. Dark walls of swirling dirt reached
into the sky as miles of topsoil lifted up in blinding clouds. The soil on the Pea
Farm became what Arkansans call "buckshot clay." Hoeing the rows stirred
up choking dust across the flat expanse. The entire prison farm consisted of
a few squat, narrow barracks; some sheds for mules, hogs and chickens; a
water tower; and a two-story farmhouse. Jacksonville is located just across the
Arkansas River from the capital city of Little Rock, but the Pea Farm was so
dislocated from civilization it might as well have been on the moon.

Beyond the prison fields stretched the tree line and a skinny dirt road. The only shade on the property was provided by a large oak in front of the farmhouse where Mr. and Mrs. Brockman lived. Mrs. Brockman was warden of the women's prison; her husband's title was "assistant superintendent." Helen joined the few dozen other inmates working in the fields, where they were guarded by a prison trusty, a man named Frank Martin. Serving a twenty-one-year sentence for shooting and killing an unarmed man, Frank Martin was now allowed to carry a gun. He was the sole guard on staff at the Pea Farm.

The date of Helen's confession coincides with Bonnie and Clyde's arrival in Arkansas. The Barrow Gang holed up for a week, hiding out in a roadside "tourist camp" in Fort Smith after a spree of kidnappings, robbery and murder. Newspapers published front-page photographs of a gun-toting Bonnie Parker. Posing next to Clyde's getaway car, a cigar clenched between her teeth and a foot propped on the running board, Bonnie Parker's image defined a gangster's moll. The pictures, along with several poems that Bonnie wrote, had been found after the gang's narrow escape from a shootout in Missouri. A cult of personality grew around Bonnie and Clyde. Stories spread of the young couple's impoverished beginnings and of Clyde Barrow's stint in a notorious Texas prison and his vow of revenge against the Lone Star State's corrupt penitentiary system. After robbing a grocery store and killing an Arkansas marshal, the Barrow Gang fled Fort Smith and disappeared again.

June 1933 also saw Arkansas outlaw Frank "Jelly" Nash meet his undoing. Federal Bureau of Investigation (FBI) agents tracked the sometime safecracker for Ma Barker's Gang to a lakeside hideout in Hot Springs. He was captured and scheduled for transport by train to Kansas City, Missouri. Word got around, and several gangsters (including Pretty Boy Floyd, according to FBI accounts) moved to intercept the lawmen. When the train pulled into the station, the gangsters launched an ambush. The Kansas City Massacre, so-called for the four FBI agents killed, also claimed the life of "Jelly" Nash.

Throughout that long, hot summer, Helen worked like a machine from dawn to dusk, her olive skin turning brown as a bean. After dinner in the mess hall, the exhausted women filed back to the barracks. In the evenings, the low-ceilinged room became a place of storytelling and shared confidences as the inmates sought to pass the time. A federal prisoner named Catherine took Helen under her wing, and a friendship blossomed.

"Tell us about the river, Helen," was a request repeated nightly along the row of cots. The women never tired of hearing about life on the White River. Helen's vivid tales of swim parties, fish fries and barbecues made the listeners sigh and their stomachs growl. The girl tried to describe the smell of the river, its green perfume and honeysuckle breath. The women heard all about the folks of Arkansas County. Any story about "the Jenkins Boys" was an instant favorite.

"The Jenkins Boys go to the dry-lander church," Helen would begin as the candle was snuffed out for the night.

> *Folks come from miles around in buckboard wagons like big shoeboxes on wheels. They tie up the horses in the shade. If a baby starts crying during Preacher Burton's sermon, the mother takes it outside, bundles it up and tucks it in back o' the wagon. Baby just sleeps, stowed away in the buckboard 'til church lets out at noontime.*
>
> *One Sunday morning, the Jenkins Boys switched all those babies around. When folks got home to Sunday dinner, nobody had the right baby. They had to turn right around and take 'em all where they belonged. After a couple Sundays of this, those dry-landers got wise and took to checking their babies before they left the church.*

Muffled giggles, and then Helen would commence another:

> *The Jenkins Boys like to sit in the back pew of the dry-lander church. One Sunday morning, Preacher Burton was sermonizing, and the Jenkins Boys start to scuffing their boots on the floor, drowning 'im out. Well, Preacher Burton doesn't say anything, but the next time he shows up to preach, he unpacks his Bible and lays it on the pulpit. He takes out his pocket watch and puts that beside. Then he pulls out his pistol and sets that down too, and he says: "I come here to preach the Word of the Lord. But if anybody in back wants to make noise—I'll be happy to send 'im to Hell!"*

Snorts of laughter would trail off until, one by one, the women escaped for a while into the oblivion of sleep.

Because Catherine was a federal prisoner awaiting transfer, she enjoyed certain privileges. She didn't have to work in the fields, for example, and her movements around the Pea Farm were somewhat less restricted. She worked at the Big House, typing up various official forms and correspondence for Mrs. Brockman to sign. Catherine was adept at eavesdropping on the Brockmans and shared with the others whatever news she overheard. It came to pass that Catherine learned of an impending scheme: some of the younger girls were to be taken by bus to Memphis and forced to sleep with men in exchange for money. Arrangements were being made, Catherine said. These tidings cast a divisive pall over the barracks. Some of the women angrily denounced Catherine for spreading fear and lies, while others brooded in silence. Catherine and Helen, wide awake in their cots, whispered late into the night.

Summer blazed into fall, and still the prisoners waited to see if Catherine's stark revelation would come true. Pulp magazines and paperback novels called such a thing "white slavery." So what if the Pea Farm was broke?

Arkansas prisons had always been underfunded—a situation made worse by the Depression. The penitentiary system's agricultural foundations were shattering under drought and dropping prices. When the federal government proposed repeal of prohibition, Arkansas went along and ratified the Twenty-first Amendment on August 1, 1933, if only for economic reasons. Governor Futrell was under constant pressure to raise revenues; he responded by slashing state programs and supporting legalization of gambling. Futrell eventually went so far as to promote the "Convict Corn Plan," which sought to turn Arkansas penitentiaries into whiskey distilleries.

President Franklin D. Roosevelt stepped in with the creation in 1933 of the Civilian Conservation Corps (CCC). The CCC offered a Depression-era first: something tangible to destitute Americans. Jobs and housing were guaranteed for workers building roads, large-scale infrastructure and soil conservation projects. From tree planting to firefighting to constructing state parks, bridges and buildings using native Ozark stone, the CCC provided a creative solution to Arkansas' joblessness and hunger. Besides, the state was technically bankrupt. Governor Futrell, for all his insistence on self-help, embraced this New Deal from FDR and made certain to steer his political supporters into positions of authority within the CCC.

On the afternoon of September 13, Helen was digging sweet potatoes when she stood and stretched, staring into the distance. A Great Blue Heron flapped slowly over the treetops. The other girls paid no attention at first, but soon a ripple of tension ran down the line as everyone noticed at the same time: she's leaving! Helen was escaping—or rather, walking away. The Pea Farm being unaccustomed to escapes, its fencing was altogether hodgepodge. Helen had spotted a hole in the perimeter wire fence, and the effect was magnetic. Without looking back, the girl broke into a run.

An alarm bell sounded, and the women returned to the barracks, talking excitedly. One girl took nickel bets on Helen's chances of getting clean away. A distraught Catherine paced the floor; others prayed. Three hours passed before word came that Helen had been found and returned to the Pea Farm. Catherine ran out the door toward the main farmhouse, where she caught up with Mr. Brockman by the oak tree. The girls watched from the barracks window as Catherine pleaded with the man. He shook his finger in her face and pointed to the barracks. Catherine returned and collapsed on her cot. It was some time before the others could make any sense of what she was saying.

"Ten lashes! Ten lashes," Catherine kept repeating. "Helen's too tiny—they're gonna kill her with the blacksnake!" The women gathered in a huddle on the opposite side of the room, where some demanded to know what Catherine was yammering about. One of the older inmates explained that a blacksnake was a long leather strop. The prisoner was

69

stripped naked, placed spread-eagled over a wooden barrel—the origin
of the phrase "you've got me over a barrel"—and flogged.

Suddenly, Frank Martin was standing in the doorway. He motioned for
Catherine to follow him. The women jostled at the window, watching as the pair
walked to the Big House and took the cement steps down into the basement.

The cellar's windowless anteroom contained a desk and typewriter. As Frank
Martin stood watch, Catherine dutifully typed up the report dated September
13, 1933. Under "Description of Convict," she plunked out the following:

> *Age when convicted: 18.*
> *Color: White.*
> *Complexion: Fair.*
> *Height: 5'1".*
> *Shoe size: 5½.*
> *Weight: 135.*
> *Sex: Female.*

The report, addressed to the Arkansas Penitentiary Board in Little Rock,
bears the usual salutation, "Gentlemen," and then reads as follows:

> *I have today corrected Helen Spence*
> *Register No. 127*
> *Crime: Murder 2nd Degree*
> *Term: 10*
> *Color: White*
> *County: Arkansas*
> *For what offense corrected: For Escaping*
> *How corrected: 10 Lashes*

The smack of leather slamming into flesh and Helen's screams sounded
from the next room. Finally, the door opened, and Mr. and Mrs. Brockman
entered. Where Catherine had typed the closing line, "Yours truly," Mrs.
Brockman signed her name in a flowing script. Her husband took the pen
and made his signature, "V.O. Brockman," beneath the word "Witness."
After ordering Catherine to help Helen get her clothes back on, the couple
went upstairs to supper. Frank Martin escorted the women back to the
barracks, Helen leaning heavily on Catherine's arm.

Chapter 8

A Series of Daring Escapes

The Brockmans had "corrected" Helen, but if the couple thought her spirit was broken, they were dead wrong. Back on the line after a few days' recuperation from the flogging, Helen spied another hole in the fence and escaped again on September 18. This time, she made it all the way to the banks of the Arkansas River. Born in the mountains of Colorado, the Arkansas River nevertheless shares the Quapaw territorial name. Wide, deep and muddy, the Arkansas has more in common with the Mississippi than with the White River. Crossing the center of the state, the Arkansas is a thing of monstrous beauty and deadly force. Whirlpools, undertows and shifting sandbars make swimming the height of folly. The river barred Helen's path; the roads were being watched.

The women at the Pea Farm waited uneasily for news. When Helen was recaptured the following day, spirits fell. Catherine voiced dread at the prospect of being called again to the Big House. But to everyone's surprise, the call did not come. No records have been found to tell what sort of "correction" took place in the Brockmans' cellar room. Whatever occurred there, the outcome was dire: Helen contracted a fever, perhaps from a kidney infection. She lay in her cot unable to walk, sinking into delirium. A week passed, and the infection went systemic. The girl's condition was alarming enough that someone at the prison sent a message to DeWitt. It appeared Helen might die.

A letter to the prison dated October 4, 1933, inquires about her state. Sent by DeWitt lawyer J.M. Brice on behalf of Helen's uncle, Pless Spence, the typewritten letter is addressed to the superintendent of the State Farm for Women and bears the salutation "Dear Friend:"

> *After receiving your message, I phoned to some of Mr. Spence's friends at St. Charles and they said that they would endeavor to get a message to him at once. I have not seen or heard from him. The only way to reach him is by the river route, at this time.*

The letter goes on to give Helen's sister Edie's last known address in Oklahoma and concludes:

> *Of course, her relatives and friends here would like to know about her illness, what kind of disease is affecting her, how long she has been sick and what progress she is making toward recovery. I beg to remain*
>
> *Yours truly,*
> *J.M. Brice*

Whether Mr. Brice received any reply from the Pea Farm is unknown, but handwritten prison records detail Helen's 'round-the-clock medical care—or rather, ordeal. For days, the girl languished in the Pea Farm's primitive medical ward. Records show that sodium benzoate was prescribed, a medicine once used to treat high levels of ammonia in the bloodstream—an indication of kidney damage and potential organ failure. Helen was also prescribed the heart medication digitalis "every four hours when pulse is above 130." Her condition was updated every few minutes at first, and between the hours of 4:00 p.m. and 6:00 p.m. on September 30, the girl was given no fewer than five enemas. One of these treatments is recorded as "a high enema with a colon tube."

The medieval treatments continued. Helen slipped into a "coma" on October 2 after more rounds of enemas (now joined by repeated douches), as well as a significant amount of morphine (one and a half grams in less than three hours). Still, the girl's fever remained above 101 degrees. By the morning of October 3, the medical staff was using half-pints of "sweet milk" in the ongoing series of enemas. Additional morphine was prescribed; Helen was subjected all that day to nonstop rounds of douches, enemas and morphine injections. Her fever rose to 103 degrees.

The physician for the women's prison, Dr. E.H. Abington, contacted his superiors. That night, the superintendent of Arkansas' prison system, A.G.

Stedman, arrived to personally transport Helen to a hospital in the small town of Beebe, Arkansas, north of Jacksonville. Over the next two days, her fever began to recede, and she was given tablets of something called "Alumnol," possibly a trade name for a product containing alum, which induces vomiting. Helen remained in the hospital until the afternoon of October 7, when she was transported back to the Pea Farm. It is recorded that she "arrived at Institution in very good condition."

Meanwhile, back in Arkansas County, plenty of folks were wondering about Helen's condition. Rumors spread among the River People; the community's growing sense of alarm prompted John Black to meet with Sheriff Lem. Sheriff Lem listened sympathetically but could offer John no advice beyond staying as informed as possible. At night, sitting at the kitchen table with Mrs. Brown, Lem voiced frustration over the whole sad state of affairs. The Browns conversed at length, unaware that L.C., concealed on the upstairs landing, heard every word. The boy did not understand some of the phrases his parents used, but he knew full well that something was terribly wrong.

Due to Helen's escapes, she was no longer allowed to work in the fields. She gradually recovered her strength and began working in the prison laundry. Catherine still spoke of an upcoming trip to Memphis for purposes of prostituting the younger prisoners, but the other women disregarded her warnings. With the passage of time, the inmates had grown complacent. They scoffed at Catherine, calling her a fear-monger and rabble-rouser. Helen, however, listened intently to everything Catherine said. The girl began spending hours each night sewing by candlelight, refusing to show anyone her handiwork. Often, she and Catherine whispered together long after the others had fallen asleep.

Thanksgiving of 1933 stands out in L.C.'s mind, not because the Brown family meal was especially memorable but for what he overheard his parents say when the rest of the family was in bed. Stretched out on the upstairs landing unobserved with his pillow and blanket, the boy once again listened to the low voices coming from the kitchen. His parents were talking about John Black.

"John just got the story, and he's pretty upset about it," Lem was saying as L.C.'s mother finished up the dishes. She murmured something the boy didn't catch; the sound of a chair pulling up to the table meant that she was done for the night.

"A few days ago," Lem began, "the warden had a bus come out to the prison and take some of the girls over to Memphis. Miz Brockman—well, lemme just say the plan was to make the girls turn tricks. Aw Stella, don't cry!" L.C. waited while his father took a minute to console his mother. Grown-ups talked in code sometimes; what sort of "tricks" were these?

"So, the bus pulls into the station in West Memphis," Lem went on as Mrs. Brown sniffled in the background. "And Helen asked to use the ladies' room. Now, for the past few weeks, Helen's been working in the prison laundry. She collected a stash of those red-and-white checkered napkins—the cloth kind."

"Gingham, yes, go on," said Stella.

"So, all this time Helen's been sewing those little red-and-white cloths into the lining of her prison dress."

"She's the best seamstress in St. Charles," Stella interjected.

Lem continued, "Like I said, Helen asked to go to the restroom at the bus station. She went in there and just turned her dress inside out. She walked out of that bus station with her head held high, looking like one of those department store models. John says she made it almost to Brinkley before they caught up with her again."

L.C. had to cover his mouth to keep from laughing out loud—Helen would show those bad people! They wouldn't get the best of her, ever! The boy almost missed the rest of the story.

"So she put a stop to their plan to send those gals to Memphis, but the next day they give 'er another ten lashes with the blacksnake—aw, Stella, please don't cry."

After this latest debacle, the Brockmans appealed to Superintendent A.G. Stedman, who contacted Lieutenant Governor Lee Cazort for help with the Pea Farm's most incorrigible, unmanageable prisoner—all five feet and one inch of her. Cazort responded with a handwritten letter addressed to Stedman:

Dear Sir:

As per your request I find that inmate Helen Spence at Woman's Farm, Jacksonville, Ark., is suffering from Homocidal [sic] Mania and may be expected to attempt to kill herself or someone else at any time.
I recommend her transfer to Criminal ward at State Hospital for Nervous disease and close confinement over a period of time for observation.

Helen was taken to Arkansas' State Hospital for Nervous Diseases on December 5, 1933. On December 14, the hospital's chief of medical staff,

Dr. Charles Arkebauer, wrote to Mrs. V.O. Brockman. The brief typewritten message reads:

Re: Helen Spence

Dear Madam:
At a recent meeting of the Hospital Staff, a classification of Constitutional Psychopathic Inferiority, Without Psychosis, was made. As she is not believed to be insane, and as we are very much overcrowded and find it difficult to make room for acute and curable cases, it will be appreciated if you will return her to your Institution as soon as possible.

Yours very truly,
C. Arkebauer, M.D.

Despite the hospital's request for her transfer, Helen remained in Arkansas' version of bedlam for another two weeks before returning to the Pea Farm. She used this time to write a story and submitted the finished manuscript to a publication called *Liberty* magazine. Founded in 1906 by the Seventh-Day Adventist Church, *Liberty* magazine is dedicated to "matters of religious freedom." Helen wrote her story by hand, all forty-two pages of it, using the return address of the prison farm in Jacksonville. When the magazine sent the manuscript back a few weeks later accompanied by a rejection slip, the envelope was promptly intercepted and confiscated.

Helen's diagnosis reveals the medical advancement (or lack) of the day: "Constitutional Psychopathic Inferiority" was first described in the late 1800s by a German psychiatrist named Julius Koch. His writings caught on in the United States during the 1920s. The idea of "constitutional" meant within the makeup of a person's physical or psychological nature. The diagnosis refers to a range of neuroses including what was then (due to the effects of World War I) called "shell shock," known today as posttraumatic stress syndrome.

The catch-all phrase was shortened to "psychopathic inferiority" and eventually "inferiors." This term applied to those unable to function in society or who committed crimes. The concept of "inferiors" combined with other German psychiatric hypotheses to lay the foundations for the eugenics programs of Nazi leader Adolf Hitler. In 1930s Germany, such a diagnosis led to institutionalized citizens—including children—being starved to death for the good of the state. As time went on, these so-called "inferiors" were killed outright—the Nazi penchant for efficiency being supreme.

Helen was labeled now. The Brockmans separated her from the rest of the women in the barracks by having a wooden cage constructed especially for her. They kept her locked inside the cage, which was too small to accommodate movement. On April 4, 1934, Superintendent A.G. Stedman issued the following order:

> *In regard to Helen Spence, I do not want you to allow this subject any privilidges* [sic] *at all, except to eat in the dinning* [sic] *room where all the rest of the prisoners eat. When she has finished eating, search her, search the cell and then lock her up. I want her to be locked up all the time that she is not working. Be sure that you do not let her have any matches in the cell for I do not want her to burn it up.*

Below the typed message, Stedman added a handwritten postscript: "P.S. She must not escape."

Chapter 9

Betrayed by the State

The spring of 1934's brief flowering was smothered by summer's oncoming heat and drought. There was no end in sight to the "Dirty Thirties." As the stirrings of Nazism and fascism increased in ever-strident pitch on the other side of the globe, workers in the United States simply stopped working. Strikes spread from coast to coast; the federal government responded with drastic measures, including buying up livestock—so-called "drought cattle." The starving creatures were sent by the trainload from America's rangelands (now deserts) to hand-picked rural areas, providing food for hungry families. Some wound up in the White River bottomlands, where they did not go to waste.

A chaotic madness seized the country—it was the era of the "public enemy." Newspapers and pulp magazines multiplied breathless accounts of criminals on the rampage, from Baby Face Nelson and Pretty Boy Floyd to John Dillinger and the continuing exploits of Bonnie and Clyde.

At the Pea Farm, the women resumed the ceaseless drudgery of the fields. Helen returned to the line, where the other inmates were under strict orders not to speak to her. They kept their heads down, working mechanically. Separated from the rest of the prisoners during mealtimes, Helen was also confined in a different barracks now. Her personal, specialized cage was located in one end of the building that housed prison trusty Frank Martin. In what can only be described as an act of sheer malice, the cage was positioned near a window to receive the full force of the sun. By midday, the temperature in Helen's cell-within-a-cell climbed above one hundred degrees. The girl took to lying on the cement floor in a futile attempt to cool down.

One evening after sunset, Catherine slipped into the room housing Helen's cage only to find her friend curled in a heap on the floor. Dropping to her knees, Catherine reached through the wooden slats to take Helen's hand. The two shed tears as Catherine revealed the purpose of her visit: she had been granted a transfer and was leaving the next morning. She could only stay a minute and wanted to give Helen something to remember her by. Taking a tiny cut-glass bottle from her pocket, she placed it in Helen's palm. The perfume's delicate label bore a white flower against a green background and the words "Jungle Gardenia." Helen dabbed the amber liquid on her wrists.

"It's lovely," she whispered, "but you know I can't keep it." Handing the faceted bottle back to Catherine, Helen reached under her cot and drew forth a cardboard box containing a few personal items. She passed a Bible and a wristwatch through the bars, saying, "The watch is broken. Maybe you can get it fixed." Catherine kissed the girl's hands and was gone.

In late May, the news hit the stands: Bonnie and Clyde were dead, ambushed by lawmen on a Louisiana back road, their "death car" riddled with bullet holes and bearing a stolen Arkansas license plate. The Barrow Gang habitually made visits to family; the Texas Rangers finally mapped out the gang's comings and goings, and the routes crisscrossed Arkansas. The bodies of the infamous couple were taken back to Texas and put on public display. People came by the carload to gawk. News of Bonnie and Clyde's violent end sold 500,000 newspapers in Dallas alone. It looked to be another long, hot summer.

Helen was still taking medicine—probably digitalis. The afternoon of Tuesday, July 10, found the girl assigned to the Pea Farm's strawberry patch. Overcome by a fainting spell, she obtained permission to go to the Big House, where her medication was kept. Afterward, she walked back toward the strawberry patch. Passing it, Helen kept walking. By the time Frank Martin and V.O. Brockman shouted to her, she was already near the fence line. The girl climbed over as though the barbed wire was blackberry brambles. She darted into the woods and disappeared.

All that afternoon and evening, Helen walked, emerging from the forest after nightfall and proceeding down a dirt road. A clear night sky blazed overhead—the girl moved slowly, searching for the constellation with the belt of three bright stars, what Ada used to call "Freya's distaff" after the Norse goddess of heaven. Helen finally took shelter under a large oak. Cushioned by thick, mossy grass, she slept. In the morning, she resumed her walk down the endless dirt road. Some accounts claim that a little boy spied her as she slept under the tree; others say that Helen stopped for a drink of water at a farmhouse and got reported by a farmer's wife. The prison's posse of V.O. Brockman and Frank Martin was notified, and the men moved quickly to intercept her. Joined by Brockman's grown son, Will, the posse was armed and ready. Frank Martin carried a shotgun.

The men spotted Helen in the distance as they drove up the road. She shuffled slowly along, wearing the canvas pants and blue shirt of the field crew, her face shaded by a hat. The men stopped the car and jumped out. Hidden by a roadside hedge, Frank Martin approached Helen from behind. The *Arkansas Gazette*'s front-page story Thursday, July 12, 1934, was headlined in all caps. "NOTORIOUS GIRL FUGITIVE KILLED BY TRUSTY GUARD":

> *"I was up on the hill in the woods there," Brockman said, "when I heard the shots. They didn't sound like a shotgun to me. I thought they were pistol shots and that she had shot at Frank."*

Helen dropped to the ground, killed instantly by a single bullet that pierced the back of her head below the right ear. The *Gazette* article goes on to describe:

> *The slain girl was lying on her left side, curled up as though asleep, on the right side of the narrow road. Her large black hat had fallen off and lay beside her. The red handkerchief she wore around her neck was stained with blood.*

The *Arkansas Gazette*'s coverage of the escape and death of Helen Spence fills four pages and features several photographs. The vague account tells how she "managed somehow to unlock the door of the room occupied by the trusty guard, Martin," saying, "She stole his gun from a shelf where he habitually kept it." Witnesses at the Pea Farm later claimed that neither Martin nor V.O. Brockman made an attempt to chase Helen when she was first seen escaping. Frank Martin insisted that when he later came up behind Helen in the road, he commanded the girl "throw up her hands," but instead she "reached for a gun," the revolver she supposedly took from his room. Upon examination of Helen's body, however, it was found that

> *the gun was stuck into her clothes beneath the shirt, and the butt held in place by an undergarment.*

Her pockets were found to contain a lipstick, a nail file, a comb, a broken mirror, and a locket containing a picture of a man. Officers found nothing which might have been used to gain entrance to the trusty guard's room. She had no money with her...

...Mrs. V.O. Brockman, superintendent of the farm for women, when informed her most notorious prisoner had been slain, exclaimed:

"That is a great burden off my shoulders."

The River People read these words and beheld a larger picture: an unlocked room containing a gun as bait, a setup, a sham posse and an execution. But the *Gazette*'s front-page photo of Helen lying dead in the dirt road bears the caption: "Where Helen Spence Eaton Died in Fulfillment of Her Written Boast." This detail refers to a note found scrawled on the *Liberty* magazine rejection slip, reportedly left behind in Helen's cell. The note reads: "To whom it may concern: I'll never be taken alive!"

Publication of the note ignited a firestorm of speculation about Helen's death. This "boast" appeared to be a clumsy forgery, not handwritten evidence. Furthermore, her fatal injury (confirmed by photographs taken at the scene) was from a single bullet, not a shotgun blast at close range. Within hours, the coroner reversed his initial finding of justifiable homicide and called for a grand jury investigation. Within days, the *Gazette*'s front page featured side-by-side examples of Helen's signature juxtaposed with the discredited note. The two did not match.

A hastily convened grand jury found that Assistant Superintendent V.O. Brockman "connived in the escape" and was an accessory to the murder charged to Frank Martin. A.G. Stedman resigned from his post as superintendent of Arkansas' penal system in the resulting furor over the use of trusty guards. Mrs. Brockman also resigned and was hauled before the grand jury along with forty witnesses. A lengthy *Arkansas Gazette* article ("Two Indicted for Helen Eaton Death," July 20, 1934) describes a widening investigation into "not only the shooting...but the conduct of affairs generally at the women's farm." Trials were expected to begin in the fall. One paragraph in particular sums up the investigation's findings:

One of the reports concerning the escape and death of Helen, to which credence was lent by the indictments, was that the escape was "arranged" by Brockman and Martin and that the girl was shot deliberately to "keep her quiet."

Newspapers from Tuscaloosa to New York picked up the story of the "comely girl slayer" cut down in cold blood. Arkansas became the focus of intense negative publicity unmatched since the heyday of H.L. Mencken. One of America's foremost intellectuals, Mencken had written about the state after traveling there, blasting Depression-era Arkansas as "the apex of moronia." The state's General Assembly responded by issuing a resolution demanding an apology; however, it misspelled Mencken's name. The writer won the argument by observing that "so long as the Arkansas of today remains the Arkansas of 40 years ago, the Menckens are going to make it the butt of ridicule, and millions are going to agree with them."

As officials continued efforts to get a message to Helen's Uncle Pless somewhere on the White River, thousands of Arkansans visited the funeral parlor in North Little Rock where she lay. The *Arkansas Gazette*'s account of the spectacle, headlined, "Neglected in Life, Helen Eaton Has Become a Heroine in Death," describes offers of help pouring in. Beauty shops volunteered their services. Someone provided a silk dress; huge bouquets and sprays of flowers arrived, "most of them anonymously." The article recounts "dozens of deeds to cemetery lots" offered for Helen's final resting place, including an unnamed DeWitt woman who offered her family's burial plot, saying, "You may put her grave in the center of the lot, if you wish."

An "unusual letter" was published on the *Gazette*'s front page on July 21, 1934. Titled, "Former Friend Writes to Praise Helen Spence Eaton's Character," the letter was mailed from Winchester, Arkansas, a small Delta town. Identified only as "Mrs. Butterworth," the letter's author describes Helen as "more sweet and refined than many a girl who is raised like a queen," and notes, "I loved her like a sister":

> *Helen was loyal and true to all who were straight with her. The girls on the farm were all fond of her. She never gossiped or said mean things about them. In the room at night when the girls would gather around to gossip, Helen would be in her bed fixing her face and singing old-time songs. I have gotten in bed with her many a night to listen to her singing songs that my mother used to sing. All the time I knew her I never heard her curse.*

Helen's uncle, Blair "Pless" Spence, was located, and the remaining Spence family members prepared for her funeral. News arrived that Edie was en route from Tulsa to St. Charles, accompanied by her new husband, J.W. Ferguson. The couple carried twenty-five letters from Helen as further evidence against the forged note and told a reporter that they planned on staying on the river. They would join Edie's Uncle Pless, fishing and hunting for mussel shells.

One intrepid *Gazette* reporter interviewed Helen's grandmother, Margaret Spence, at her cottage overlooking the cemetery in St. Charles. Like most of the stories written at this time, the retelling of Helen's "brief, stormy life" is rife with inaccuracies, mistaking the date of her final escape and reporting her age as twenty-one, when other reports were claiming she was twenty-two. However, the reminiscences of Helen's grandmother ring true:

> *In the fall when the leaves are gone, I can stand in my front door and look down on my son's grave...[Helen's] mother died when [Helen] was 18 months old...[her mother] was a beautiful girl...Features, and ways like Helen, but she had very blonde hair and blue eyes.*

Helen's grandmother insisted that Helen did not kill "the Greek," explaining that the confession was just "some strange idea [Helen] had in going back and saying she did." Grandma Spence is quoted as saying, "The worst part of it all to me is that she had to be shot down like a dirty dog by a criminal." The interview concludes:

> *Mrs. Spence does not take a daily paper—says she cannot afford it and has not read all of the articles concerning her granddaughter. She saw the newspaper picture of Helen taken after she was shot down, but does not have the picture to keep, and added rather bitterly, "and I ain't a carin' for one either."*

The DeWitt lawyer, J.M. Brice, contacted the prison once more on behalf of the Spence family. He asked for Helen's few belongings; they seemed to have disappeared. His letter, dated July 30, 1934, reads:

> *Dear Madam:*
>
> *Yesterday, Mr. P.E. Spence and wife called and got the box containing the belongings of Ruth Spence Eaton. They fully appreciate your kindness in the matter, but claimed there were a few articles not forwarded. One was a locket which she usuly [sic] wore around her neck, and they are under the impression she had it on when killed. It might be the Undertaker may know something about it. Another was a Bible which was given her by a friend or paid for by a friend and delivered to her, while she was held in jail here, by*

the Baptist Minister of this place. A third article which they named was a gold wrist watch and three or four dresses, one being a cotton dress, the one she wore when before Pitcock. They also understand that she started to write her Life's History, but these were not sent, and P.E. Spence especially wants that manuscript if it can be obtained. I beg to remain
    Yours very truly,

J.M. Brice

He received this reply:

Dear Mr. Brice:

Concerning your letter of inquiry of the few articles of Helen Spence: The locket which you spoke of was on her when her body was taken to the Undertakers, and I presume that it may be recovered by going there for it, as it was never sent out here. The Bible—one of the girls here who was the closest friend Helen had—so she always said—tells me that [Helen] was given a Bible by someone and that Helen did not care to keep it and gave it to a Federal prisoner who was here at that time and the only name that she can recall was "Catherine." I am sorry that I can not give you any more definite information of that. The polka dot dress you spoke of was given to the above-mentioned girl—quite a while before she attempted her last escape. However, the girl says that she will give up the dress—if insisted upon—but we do know that Helen gave the dress to her. The other dresses we do not have any information of, as she has not been seen to have worn any others save the ones that were mailed to you...The wrist watch also was given to the federal girl prisoner "Catherine" to have repaired and was never returned to Helen. The Life History—we have no information whatever that she wrote that. She often spoke of it that she was going to, but the story that she wrote and that was rejected by the Liberty Magazine, is now in the hands of the Prosecuting Attorney—Mr. Carl Bailey—in Little Rock.

I hope that this will be a satisfactory answer to all your questions and should Mr. Spence desire any more information concerning Helen would appreciate it if he would come and talk to us.

Yours very truly,

Mrs. Ben F. Maddox, Supt.

The River People were resigned to the insult that had taken place in North Little Rock, when Helen's body was on display for public view. After all, what else could one expect from Little Rock and North Little Rock—twin cities referred to by the River People in terms of Sodom and Gomorrah. But when DeWitt's Essex Funeral Home placed Helen's body in full view framed by its wide front window and crowds began lining up around the block, it was more than the community could stand.

L.C. came in from playing to find his mother in the kitchen with his father. Estella Rebecca Brown was slamming cabinet doors, mad as a hornet about something. L.C. had never seen his mom this upset. As the bewildered boy crept slowly upstairs, Mrs. Brown cried, "They used that poor girl while she was alive—and now they're using her while she's dead. Using her body for people to stare at! Using her death to sell newspapers! It's not right, Lem, it's just not right."

L.C. ran back out of the house and around to the barn, where Wolf lay sprawled in the shade. The child hid his face in Wolf's soft fur as the hot tears came, along with the realization that Helen was truly gone. No one would see him cry.

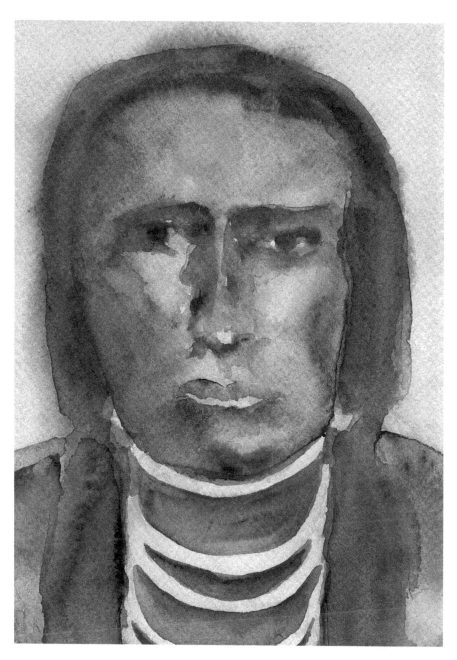

Watercolor portrait of Quapaw brave by Ellen K. White, the author's late aunt, circa 1970s. The Quapaw ("downstream people") were the original inhabitants of eastern Arkansas.

Cotter Bridge in Baxter County, Arkansas, spans a gorge of the upper White River and is an enduring example of early 1930s Art Deco design and engineering, 2007. *Photo by Mike Keckhaver.*

Opposite, top: Former houseboat-turned-saloon-turned-post office of Yancopin, Arkansas. This cypress-plank structure is the only building remaining in the now-deserted Delta town, 2007. *Photo by L.C. Brown.*

Opposite, bottom: Joe Granberry, the author's great-grandfather. An avid hunter and fisherman (as all River People were), Joe Granberry kept a houseboat at Clarendon, site of a once-thriving houseboat community, possibly circa 1940. *Courtesy of Matt White.*

Offices of the *DeWitt-Era Enterprise* newspaper, 2011. *Photo by Denise White Parkinson.*

Formerly DeWitt's Rothenhoffer Café, the building was in use as a photography studio when this 2011 photo was taken. Helen Spence worked in the café, where Jim Bohots was manager, and she lived in an upstairs apartment. *Photo by Denise White Parkinson.*

Above: DeWitt's town square on a midsummer Sunday afternoon, 2011. *Photo by Denise White Parkinson.*

Right: Cedar tree planted by John Black at Helen Spence's otherwise unmarked grave in St. Charles, 2011. *Photo by Denise White Parkinson.*

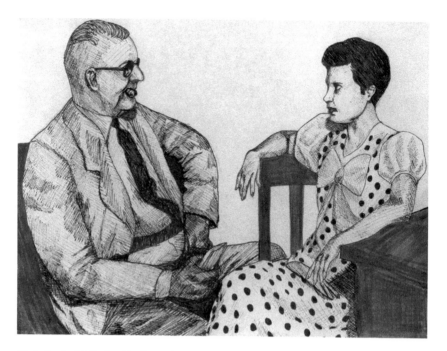

Little Rock chief of police James Pitcock had photographs made of Helen Spence's surprise confession, which came barely a week after her release from the Pea Farm (note her prison haircut). Pen and ink sketch of a photo published in *Daring Detective* magazine's September 1935 issue. *Pen and ink illustration by Grace R. Norton.*

An illustration of a large photograph of Helen Spence lying dead in the dirt road that accompanied the *Arkansas Gazette*'s July 12, 1934 front-page coverage of her escape and death at the hands of prison officials. *Pen and ink illustration by Grace R. Norton.*

Frank Martin was a convicted murderer and trusty guard at Arkansas' Women's Prison. His mug shot was published in the *Arkansas Gazette* and *Daring Detective* magazine. *Pen and ink illustration by Grace R. Norton.*

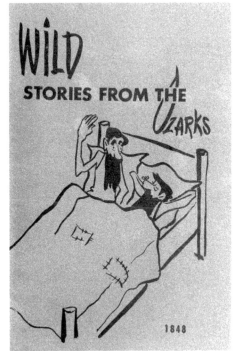

In the early 1950s, folklorist Vance Randolph published a series of pocket-sized paperback retellings of Arkansas legends that promoted negative "hillbilly" stereotypes. Issue no. 1848 of *Wild Stories from the Ozarks* contains a sensationalized bio titled "The Case of Helen Spence." *Booklet courtesy of Bob Cochran.*

old, shot right through the guts an' liable to die any minute. May be dead now, for all I know.

"Here lately they've took up shootin' at our lawyer, an' horsewhippin' folks, an' burnin' gals' feet, an' all such as that! If they keep on this way, us Henleys is liable to lose our temper. I ain't lookin' for no trouble myself," he grinned wolfishly, "but some of our young men ain't safe to project with!"

When Draper and I returned to the hotel that night, things were not so pleasant in Marshall. The town loafers knew that we were newspapermen from Kansas City, and several muttered something uncomplimentary about city slickers. After dinner we sat on a bench outside the hotel, near two men who carried Winchester carbines.

"Why all the artillery?" asked Draper.

The hillman looked at Draper contemptuously, but made no reply. A moment later one of them turned to me.

"It ain't none of your friend's business," said he. "But I got this here rifle because it ain't legal to carry a pistol. Pistols is concealed weapons," he added virtuously, "an' we're all law-abidin' citizens here in Marshall!"

The Case of Helen Spence

Cicero Spence lived in a houseboat on White River, some 60 miles east of Little Rock. He did a little trapping in the Winter, noodled catfish, rafted logs, and occasionally served as guide for a party of city sportsmen. Cicero was just an ordinary Arkansas riverman, but his daughter Helen was something else again.

Cicero's wife died when Helen was a baby, and he took the child over to Clarendon, in Monroe county, where she attended the village school until she was 12 years old. That was all the schooling Helen ever had, but she talked better than most college girls do nowadays. And she behaved better too in most situations.

Her school days over, Helen came back to White River, and lived quietly with her father on the houseboat. She did all of the cooking and housework, and learned to handle the skiff while Cicero ran his trotlines. She learned to use her father's big revolver, too. No matter how hard up Cicero was, he always bought plenty of cartridges and encouraged her to practice. "Every gal orter know how to shoot a pistol," he said, "it might come in handy some day."

At 17 Helen Spence was the prettiest girl I ever saw in my life. Black hair, snapping brown

Above: A detail of the first page of "The Case of Helen Spence." *Booklet courtesy of Bob Cochran.*

Left: The bend of the White River at St. Charles, 2011. *Photo by Denise White Parkinson.*

Oxbow lake, typical of the Arkansas Delta, near Wabbaseka, Arkansas, en route to St. Charles, 2011. *Photo by Denise White Parkinson.*

White River National Wildlife Refuge sign near St. Charles, 2011. *Photo by Denise White Parkinson.*

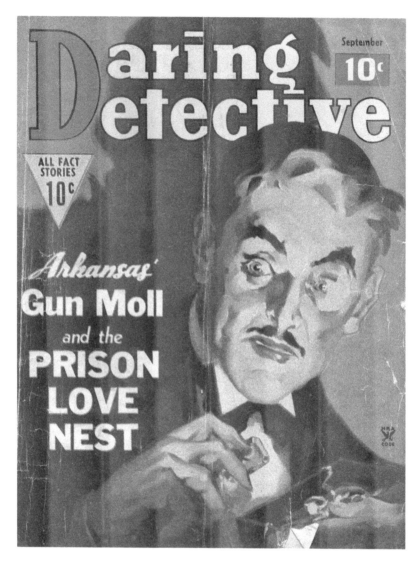

September 1935 issue of *Daring Detective*. The pulp magazine's cover story, "Arkansas' Gun Moll and the Prison Love Nest," contained no evidence of a "love nest" but did provide stunning details from grand jury testimony regarding Helen's death at the hands of prison officials. *Courtesy of the Lower White River Museum State Park, Des Arc, Arkansas.*

Opposite, top: Circa 1920s photograph of the Old DeWitt Courthouse, where Helen Spence shot Jack Worls during his trial for the murder of her father, Cicero Spence. The 1893 building was replaced with a new Art Deco–style courthouse in the 1930s. *Courtesy of the archives of the Butler Center for Arkansas Studies, Central Arkansas Library System.*

Opposite, bottom: The cedar tree at Helen Spence's grave, with view of small metal marker at adjacent grave of her father, Cicero Spence, 2011. *Photo by Denise White Parkinson.*

Above: View from the highway bridge over the White River near St. Charles, 2011. *Photo by Denise White Parkinson.*

Left: Frank and Gertrude Martin, circa late 1930s. After getting paroled, Frank Martin married and raised a large family. *Courtesy of the Lower White River Museum State Park, Des Arc, Arkansas.*

Right: Prismacolor pencil study (55" x 32") of Arkansas' largest tree, the Champion Bald Cypress at Ethel, Arkansas, by Hot Springs artist Linda Williams Palmer. The 2011 drawing is part of a statewide exhibit (Champion Trees of Arkansas: An Artist's Journey) touring throughout 2014. *Courtesy of Linda Williams Palmer.*

Below: The Champion Bald Cypress at Ethel. The tree, once a landmark for local horseracing, stands 120 feet tall and includes 10-foot-tall cypress knees (note figure in right foreground), 2011. *Photo by Linda Williams Palmer.*

Abandoned houseboat on White River near St. Charles, 2006. This houseboat appears in numerous scenes in Jeff Nichols's 2013 film *Mud*, shot on location in Arkansas County. *Photo by Nelson Chenault.*

Modern hunting club houseboat near St. Charles, 2006. *Photo by Nelson Chenault.*

Right: Monument at the crossroads in St. Charles, seen here in 2006, memorializing the White River battle with the *Mound City*, an ironclad Union gunboat, during the Civil War. The single most destructive shot of the Civil War entered the gunboat's smokestack, exploding the boiler and causing major casualties. *Photo by Nelson Chenault.*

Below: Riverside view of a modern hunting club houseboat near St. Charles, 2006. *Photo by Nelson Chenault.*

The author with her mother and sisters (Janice and twins Misti and Kristi White) during a summer visit to the White River in 1967, before the loss of the White family houseboat to flooding caused by dam releases by the U.S. Army Corps of Engineers. *Courtesy of the White family.*

Cicero Spence's grave marker at the cemetery in St. Charles. The marker, in storage for more than seventy years, was finally placed on site by DeWitt's Essex Funeral Home after L.C. Brown's efforts to bring Helen's story to light. *Courtesy of L.C. Brown.*

Above: Arkansas Women's Prison in Jacksonville, aka the "Pea Farm." Illustration from a photo published in *Daring Detective* magazine's September 1935 issue. *Pen and ink illustration by Grace R. Norton.*

Below: An illustration of a photograph of Helen Spence lying dead in the dirt road that was published in *Daring Detective*'s 1935 issue (note there are no marks of buckshot on her back). *Pen and ink illustration by Grace R. Norton.*

Image, circulated in area newspapers, depicting Helen Spence, deceased, with a pistol placed upon her dead body. *Photo courtesy of N. Boatright.*

A painting of Helen Spence, acrylic on cardboard. *Painting by Grace R. Norton.*

Chapter 10

A Reckoning

Hateful rumors proliferated after Helen's death. The worst was that she was pregnant when killed. Deputy Prosecuting Attorney Lawrence Auten requested an autopsy to quell the rumors; the results were published in the *Arkansas Gazette* on Friday, July 13, 1934. Despite the finding by five physicians that "no foundation" existed for claims that Helen was pregnant, gossip persisted. The grand jury testimony and photographs of the murder scene were obtained by a seedy "true crime" publication called *Daring Detective* magazine. Helen's handwritten memoir and the forged note, both formerly held by the prosecuting attorney's office, also wound up in the hands of the editors of *Daring Detective*.

The pulp magazine, like others of its kind popular during the Depression, represented the dregs of the exploitative "true crime" genre. A mixture of blatant fantasy and official quotes, *Daring Detective* sold for ten cents a copy. Each month, its colorful cover featured freakishly distorted portraits of deranged-looking villains and menacing, disheveled women in revealing garb.

A Delta saying goes, "even a blind hog can find an acorn once't awhile." In that sense, *Daring Detective*'s editors provided clues to Helen's murder, whether intentionally or not. The magazine's September 1935 cover story, "Arkansas' Gun Moll and the Prison Love Nest" purports to tell "the amazing life story of Helen Spence Eaton, Arkansas' most notorious gun girl." Despite such a titillating choice of title, writer Robert Barton offers only flimsy rumor of a "prison love nest," not credible evidence. The cover illustration, a dapper villain wearing a monocle, looks more Hollywood back lot than southern prison farm.

Inside is Helen's missing manuscript—or rather, the first page of her lost story. Also included are transcripts of grand jury testimony. Much of the writer's unsourced narrative serves to contradict published findings: the date of Helen's escape is wrong, as is the description of a shotgun blast rather than the fatal bullet:

> *Martin raised the 16-gauge pumpgun and sent a charge of buckshot straight into the girl's back.*

This detail is contradicted by an accompanying photograph taken at the scene that clearly shows no marks on Helen's back. The excerpted grand jury testimony, however, more than tells the tale. A scathing account of Helen's escape is included "that threw more light on that portion of the weird affair than any other." An eyewitness, Ed Williams, had come to fix the Pea Farm's water pump. Barton emphasized that Williams's grand jury deposition "is copied word for word from the court records." The transcript, published with V.O. Brockman's name redacted, refers to Brockman as "X_____":

> *Mr. Williams stated that he was working in the pump house at the Women's State Farm, together with X_____ and Frank Martin on the afternoon that Helen Spence Eaton escaped. That during that time they were working Frank Martin left several times, going after water and possibly other things.*
>
> *He did not recall on what errand Martin left when he discovered Helen's escape but said he had been gone possibly ten minutes when he returned and told X_____ that Helen was leaving.*
>
> *X_____ said: "Stop her."*
>
> *Martin said: "I'll stop her."*
>
> *He left on a run, going toward his room. X_____ went out the door of the pump house, which faces north, and Williams went after him. X_____ called to Helen to stop but she did not pay any attention to him. At this point Helen was about 150 yards out in the field walking slowly in a northeasterly direction towards a thicket.*
>
> *X_____ called to her again to stop, and said something—Williams could not recall exactly what—about shooting her. She turned and said something unintelligible and pointed towards a thicket and turned again and started walking in that direction.*
>
> *X_____ ran from the pump house toward the northeast corner of the fenced in area and disappeared from Williams' sight. Martin appeared at this point and hollered, "She got my gun."*

Williams did not know what X_____ told Martin then, or where Martin went. He could see Helen, who continued to walk a short way and then broke into a slow trot.

X_____ came into a [sic] view very shortly, running across the fields outside the enclosure, following Helen. He came in sight about a hundred yards out in the field. Helen continued until she got to a fence and climbed over it. In doing so, she caught her clothes and took a minute getting loose.

When she got over the fence she turned, and placing her arms on the top of the fence looked back for possibly a minute, maybe a little less. X_____, of course, was still running in her direction.

She turned and disappeared in a thicket at a walk. X_____ did not go to the exact point where she disappeared in the woods, but was down the fence about forty or fifty yards.

He stopped there and looked into the woods for a short space of time and then turned and came back to the buildings. Martin, in the meantime had come out of the house with Will X_____ (son). He had a shotgun and a revolver and wanted to give the revolver to Martin. Martin would not take it, saying he wanted the shotgun.

Will X_____ gave Martin the shotgun but Martin did not know how to load it and gave it back to Will, who loaded it for him and showed him how to shoot it.

Martin took the gun and started off on a run, saying, "I'll kill the ---- -." X_____ returned to the pump house and told Williams that he could have caught Helen if she had not had the gun as he could hear her crashing through the underbrush when he got to the fence.

Martin disappeared into the woods after Helen. Williams said that X_____ appeared cool and unexcited all the time, but that Martin appeared highly nervous and very excited.

Whatever else it may have done, *Daring Detective's* cover story revealed the inner workings of the Pea Farm, as evidenced by inclusion of the memo from former superintendent A.G. Stedman ("She must not escape"), as well as testimony by Dr. E.H. Abington concerning Helen's mystery illness:

She said she had a severe pain in her chest like something had torn loose, and that was immediately followed by an attack of the heart, and she was at the point of death for a number of days.

I told her never to try to run away again, that if she did the probabilities were that her heart would stop in her effort to climb some of those hills or fences in that section...About three weeks later I was called to see her again. She had another heart attack. She was in this cell. I wish you men could see that cell.

The grand jury transcript does not include Dr. Abington's description of Helen's cell, but the doctor's autobiography, *Back Roads and Bicarbonate*, was excerpted in later accounts to reveal the dimensions of the specialized cage:

She was in the west end of the building in a room about six by ten feet. There was one door and one small window. The temperature inside the room was not less than 105 degrees.

When Dr. Abington had ordered that Helen be removed from the cell, prison staff quoted the instructions of A.G. Stedman. The doctor wrote in his memoir:

I picked her up, put her on my shoulder, carried her across the yard, and put her on a bed in the main building.

Dr. Abington then told officials at the Pea Farm:

If you think there is any danger of her running away, you have my permission to put a ball and chain on her, but don't you put her back in that room.

Daring Detective's story concludes with the state's disposition of the case, in which Frank Martin was tried first for the murder charge. A technicality of Arkansas state law acquitted Martin of murdering Helen Spence:

Section 9691—Combination to escape—Authority of guards... And if said officers or guards employed in said penitentiary or any of them, shall in the attempt to prevent the escape of any convict, or any attempt to retake any convict who shall have escaped, or in the attempt to suppress any riot, revolt or insurrection, take the life of any convict, such officer or guard shall not be held responsible therefor unless the same is done UNNECESSARILY OR WANTONLY.

With Martin's acquittal, further charges against V.O. Brockman were dismissed. The glaring inconsistencies regarding the fatal pistol shot were never resolved. The investigation was closed without the state exploring the hierarchy beyond the Brockmans and prison superintendent A.G. Stedman. All three were accorded the worst that could happen to employed persons during the Great Depression: they lost their jobs.

Frank Martin was eventually paroled; he went on to marry and raise a large family. He developed a reputation as a strict—sometimes brutal—disciplinarian, but his children turned out fine. A former neighbor recalled playing with his daughters and said that it was an unspoken tenet: "Frank Martin was told that if he shot her, he could get out of prison."

Martin spent the rest of his life working as a tenant farmer near DeValls Bluff; he died at his home after battling cancer and is buried in Biscoe, Arkansas. A legend grew around Frank Martin too: that he had gone to buy bread at Cloud's Grocery near DeValls Bluff and that the lady at the counter sold him a different loaf, saying it cost less and was just as good. When Frank Martin ate dinner that night and didn't wake up the next morning, River People merely shrugged at the news, saying, "The river got him."

Helen's literary attempts were noted by journalists covering her story, and an *Arkansas Gazette* article ("Helen Spence Eaton's Career in Crime Unique in State's History," July 12, 1934) attributes two poems to Helen, verses discovered "in the specially built cage that has been her home since psychiatrists declared she was not insane." However, the first poem was immediately debunked: two Little Rock ministers pointed out that the verses were actually a song from a hymnal ("Lord, We Come Before Thee Now"), written in 1745.

The second poem published by the *Gazette* and attributed to Helen is not so easily explained. Titled "Echoes," the rhyme is of unknown origin and described as going on for many verses. The *Gazette* excerpted it:

Now, this is no secret ambition of mine
It's merely to occupy some of the time.
You can't heal the heart with no work for the hand
So I pick up my pencil and do what I can.
I'd rather be plowing or chopping down brush
Or rowing a boat in your Arkansas slush
Or scrubbing the fleas from a tiny fox dog
Or sawing and hauling a big hickory log
Or dodging the ruts in a bumpy old Ford
With oodles of kiddies on each running board
And picking them up at each turn in the road

Till Lizzy called Henry to help with her load.
Or riding the trail on an old lazy mare
Now and then chasing a cotton tail hare
Here and there ducking a nut thrown at me
By a nibbling squirrel that will chuckle and flee…
…So here by my window I dream of it all
When shadows like these come and play on the wall
And out of the wreckage I'm forced to confess
I might build again and perhaps for the best.

As for Helen's lost manuscript page, it could be considered a voice from beyond the grave. Written and signed in cursive, it appears on page ten of *Daring Detective* and is the only surviving fragment thought to have been left by Helen:

Relative to Iniquity

On the southeast coast, about twenty miles out from San Francisco bay, a one hundred and seventy-nine ft. schooner was anchored. From within the cabin came a faint metallic clinking of poker chips between curses and raucous laughter.

While out on deck the moon filtered through the foggy mist and fell on the blond hair of a tall girlish figure. Like a Norse goddess she stood erect, face lifted and silent.

Her demeanor as she stood eagerly inhaling the salty sea breeze expressed that of a small bird which has been temporarily released from captivity. Lillian Rubynov had for the moment forgotten the sordidness of the stuffy liquor and tobacco-scented rooms.

A step sounding behind her broke into the silent reverie. Slowly turning, she faced Ralph Campan [spelling illegible]. The girl had been so engrossed in thought as to not hear him emerge from the cabin behind…

This fragment joins a clipping that John Black kept, an undated *DeWitt Era-Enterprise* editorial published after Helen's death:

HELEN SPENCE BURIED AT ST. CHARLES

The funeral services of Helen Spence were held at St. Charles Sunday afternoon at 2:30 o'clock. Her remains were buried beside her father for whom she had an attachment that was sublime. Hundreds from far and near attended the services. Many flowers were sent, and hundreds called at the undertaking parlor to view the remains.

The writer or writers recounted the saga of Helen Spence, echoing local sentiment by declaring, "[Jim] Bohot's [*sic*] record was bad. Any good lawyer could have cleared her on her own statement," and concluding that "she was doubtless demented or it was through a religious feeling that she confessed to the killing of Bohot. She was free and there was no need or excuse for it."

A mixture of opinion, reportage, biography and obituary, the lengthy article reports, "The killing and shot in the back of the head aroused statewide resentment. It has resulted in a shakeup at the penitentiary and a complete change in management." The closing paragraph reads:

Respectable people who knew her in childhood tell us that they never saw a more reserved, ladylike child. They said that when a rough crowd went to her father's boat, she never mingled among them but went to her room and there remained. It is often a puzzle to know what to do in such cases. She was a fit subject for study, and the result might have been very different, had she been placed with good people clear away from all she had ever known. She might have become a good woman. We felt the feeling of remorse the same as many others upon the news of her death. It is sad, lamentable and baffling.

L.C. Brown left the family farm at the age of seventeen after getting permission from his parents to join the army. He wanted to see the world beyond the Arkansas Delta. His father told Mrs. Brown not to worry about Junior going off to World War II. "That boy is woods-smart, Stella," Lem said. And so L.C., with his "Eye-talian" and German-speaking skills, was swept into the ranks of the Pathfinders. He spent World War II parachuting behind enemy lines, tracking down spies and "fumigating" enemy camps. A teenage sharpshooter, he traded the target of fox squirrels for Nazis.

"I came home on leave, and Dad told me how Wolf died," L.C. recalls. "When I left, Wolf refused to eat. He snarled at anyone who tried to come near. Dad had to shoot him so he wouldn't die of starvation."

L.C.—on leave and in uniform—wandered into a DeWitt café and caught the eye of a vivacious brunette named Anna Grace. The two fell in love, married and left the Delta. The Browns came to the hills of Hot Springs, a place of lakes and rivers, and called it home. They raised two strapping sons and a daughter, also tall, a skilled horsewoman. L.C. still carried a gun, but for the Hot Springs Police Department. But that is a story for another day.

Arkansas' corrupt prison system continued like a dry rot until the late 1960s, when a reform effort uncovered the use of the "Tucker Telephone," named for Tucker Prison Farm. This invention consisted of an old-fashioned crank telephone wired in sequence with two batteries. Electrodes were attached from it to a prisoner's big toe and genitals; a "long-distance call" was prison slang for the torture. A book resulted from the reform attempt, *Accomplices to the Crime: The Arkansas Prison Scandal* by Joe Hyams and Thomas O. Murton, published in 1970. A film version followed, 1980's *Brubaker*, starring Robert Redford. From 1981 to 1982, Arkansas' prisons were deemed unconstitutional by the Eighth Circuit Court of Appeals. After the court ceased oversight, another prison scandal shamed the state. An investigation revealed that Arkansas prison officials had knowingly collected HIV-infected blood from prisoners and sold it around the world. In 1994, Arkansas became the last state in the United States to stop selling blood taken from prisoners.

The River People survived by closing ranks and embracing a code of silence. The community demanded privacy in the absence of respect for their way of life. The bond of trust between riverman and dry-lander was broken. The lower White River became a giant CCC floating camp, and large-scale building projects began in the Delta, with CCC recruits constructing boats, roads, levees and bridges. After the CCC disbanded, the U.S. Army Corps of Engineers was given dominion over the White River. The Corps began decades of dam-building and destructive dredging; its military-style occupation of the South's most fertile bottomland continues to this day.

Beginning in the mid-1930s, untold numbers of Delta families were forced from their homes. An organization called the Southern Tenant Farmers' Union sprang up with the goal of improving working conditions for sharecroppers; membership in the STFU guaranteed eviction. Tenant farmers and sharecroppers who dared unionize were kicked off plantations, often at the point of a gun.

The diaspora continued with the establishment of the White River National Wildlife Refuge. Facing eviction by government officials, the White River's houseboat families slowly disappeared. Edie and her husband, J.W., drifted into the past, together with Uncle Pless, Uncle Archie, Grandma Spence and all who kept the code of River Justice, who understood what it means when "the river gets in your blood."

Chapter 11

Forget Me Not

A red cedar grows in the far corner of a lonesome cemetery in the small southeast Arkansas town of St. Charles. Through drought, flood, wind, ice storm and unto drought again, the tree remains. The red cedar is about eighty years old. We know the reason it was planted, as well as the name of the man who planted it: John Black. It was uprooted in the first year of growth, knee-high and wild, from the banks of the nearby White River, which moves green and wide around a deserted bend deep enough to float a barge. The cedar was taken under cover of night to its present location, where it shades a cemetery that bears no name or signage; even the church has disappeared. The tree stands to a current height of about fifty feet.

John Black planted it there on a summer night in 1934. In those days in Arkansas, when someone died a violent or scandalous death (whether by misfortune or their own hand), no headstone was placed to mark the grave. Instead, a cedar or other native tree was planted. The origins of this burial custom are lost. Native Americans consider the cedar sacred; also, because many Arkansas settlers came from the British Isles—families with surnames like Black and Brown and White—the tradition could have arrived from England, Wales, Scotland and Ireland. The practice may recall Celtic beliefs of long ago, when trees and rivers still spoke to humankind.

John Black dug a hole in the rich Delta earth and planted the tree to mark the burial place of Helen Ruth Spence. He had carried the girl's lifeless body to this patch of ground miles away from the Essex Funeral Home in the Arkansas County seat of DeWitt, Arkansas. He did this with the help of others, who waited with him until dark to enter the funeral home in stealth and spirit away the body lying within.

They were of one mind that night: to foil the gawking crowds that arrived in droves and stood in line for hours to peer in at the dead girl, laid out in a hastily built coffin before the funeral home's wide front window. She had lain there already a night and a day: Helen Spence—so young, beautiful even in death, a so-called outlaw murdered at the hands of the state. And why shouldn't she be an outlaw, being as she was of the river? For Helen Spence (like John Black and the ones who helped take her away) belonged to the River People. A breed extinct as the ancient Celts and for similar reasons: they were mortally fond of freedom.

"It took me three trips to St. Charles before John Black told me why he called me out to his place," L.C. said. L.C. Brown is nearly ninety years old. He has told the story of Helen and the River People before and will continue to do so as long as he has breath in his body. It cost him dearly in the beginning among the stern-eyed men and women of the area who still remembered Helen Spence and heard the story passed down over the years. They had kept the secret of her death for so long that at first they were angry when L.C. told. But they forgave him, and now they wait to see who listens.

"I was living in Hot Springs in the late 1970s, and I went down to John's place one time, then two times, and all we did was talk and go fishing," L.C. recalled. "He fixed some dinner for us, and then I headed home. Finally, John calls me again to come see him. I went to his place and just sat there staring at him. 'John,' I says, 'why did you ask me to come out here? It's a three-hour drive both ways, and I don't enjoy your cooking that much.'"

L.C. followed his childhood friend to the cemetery and listened as John recalled the intervening years since Helen was killed. In 1935, the year after her death, the federal government passed a law creating the Lower White River Wildlife Refuge. The government began evicting houseboat families, banning the River People from the refuge's 160,000 acres of fertile bottomland. The only exceptions to this law were gentlemen's hunting clubs. The exclusive hunt clubs were allowed to keep their houseboats and racked up a loyal membership of doctors, lawyers and politicians. The whole area became a game preserve, a swampy Sherwood Forest, albeit a capitalistic one—permits to hunt the king's deer were sold to the highest bidder.

John was in his twenties when Helen died. Since then, he'd moved off the river into St. Charles, found a wife, worked a job and raised children. Over time, he had dwindled back to just himself: a slender, still dark-haired man bent with age, living in a small wood-frame house near a nameless cemetery in a fading southern town.

"He knew he was dying," L.C. explained, "and that he had to entrust the secret to someone, so he called me. John never told anybody exactly where Helen was buried. I don't think he even told his wife. Anyone who might have known is dead and gone. John says to me, 'This is why I'm telling you now.'"

Helen and her father lay buried side by side in an out-of-the-way spot. Neither grave was marked. John Black volunteered to be caretaker of the whole cemetery so he could tend Helen's grave. For half a century, he cut the grass and disposed of bouquets of flowers when they lost their bloom. He waited until the moon was out to carry water to the cedar tree. Every year on Helen's birthday, after sunset, John took one flower from each of the bouquets at other headstones. He placed the flowers at Helen's resting place, together with whatever wildflowers he had picked. Before sunrise, he would come back and gather them up, replacing the borrowed flowers one by one in their respective vases. The date of Helen's birth remains a mystery—this knowledge must have died with John.

L.C. Brown keeps a collection of yellowed newspaper clippings given for safekeeping by John Black. A headline in all-capital letters—"Girl Slayer, Freed, Plans New 'Start'"—marks one article. Two of the stories feature the same photograph of Helen, an up-close snapshot of her elfin face, her pixie-ish dark-brown bob suggesting a 1920s flapper. On rectangles of brittle yellow newsprint, edges turning to dust, Helen's smile is brilliant and unfading. Her deep brown eyes glance slightly upward as though she stares at someone standing just beyond the photographer's shoulder, someone she knows and admires.

Together with the newspaper articles, John gave L.C. several actual photographs of Helen. In one, she is about five years old, seated on the wooden stoop of what appears to be a barn or general store. Helen's father, Cicero, kneels beside, holding his pistol pointed downward and away, while John Black kneels close by. Several other grinning little boys kneel beside John, hands thrust into pockets of their buckskin coats. John appears to be about eight years old and gazes intently into the camera. Helen, perched on the bench with her legs dangling, glances from beneath dark curls toward John Black. She clutches what appears to be a rag doll; Helen's white stockings are tucked into dainty black ankle boots (L.C. explained that her stockings are long johns). It must be autumn or winter because Cicero wears a hat, long sleeves and a vest studded with shotgun shells sewn in little pockets. John's gloves are several sizes too large.

This black-and-white photograph, a study of pre-Depression Arkansas, depicts row upon row of raccoon and fox pelts spread on cane frames nailed to the rough-hewn, unpainted wall. Powder horns hang from pegs by strips of leather; a large deerskin is stretched across part of the wall. The antlered head of a six-point buck is evident on the bench next to Helen. A black hound dog with a white blaze on its chest looks on, next to an unnamed hunter.

L.C. keeps this photograph and the old newspaper articles inside a locked briefcase together with two other photos of Helen. Taken when she was in her teens, the pictures show her posed alongside a thin, cocky-looking young man with a hand-rolled cigarette in his mouth and a rakish tilt to his hat. His wide tie contrasts clownishly with his striped shirt; he stands hand on hip, glowering. His name is Buster Eaton, and Helen was married to him, briefly, before she left to rejoin her family at their houseboat on the White River.

Buster was a moonshiner, and his aspect suggests a Clyde Barrow–like air, while Helen appears nothing like images of gun-toting Bonnie Parker. Instead, Helen grins impishly beneath a cloche hat, slender in a hand-sewn cotton print dress with tiers of tiny ruffles on the sleeves and a skirt that falls below the knee. She poses with Buster against a large wood-framed structure, a contraption once used for weighing cotton to be loaded onto paddle-wheelers. The posy pattern on Helen's white dress softens the portrait.

L.C. also treasures a pair of rare freshwater pearls called "River Tears." The twin pearls came from the same mussel, part of a Depression-era haul out of the White River. The symmetrical pearls have been fashioned into teardrop earrings that L.C. keeps in a box inside his desk drawer. "The man that gave me these pearls was my neighbor, George Williams; he pulled 'em from the shell—he never sold 'em. Two river tears from the same shell was bad luck, George used to say. This was before the mussels played out," L.C. muttered. "Before they built the Dam."

River People call it "the Dam," and the way they pronounce the words suggests a proper noun. The reference is to Bull Shoals Dam on the upper White River. The Dam changed everything on the lower White River. Initiated by the federal Flood Control Act of 1938, Bull Shoals Dam is described in official state reports as containing 2.1 million cubic yards of concrete. Its powerhouse was, for a time, the largest building in Arkansas. Upon construction, Bull Shoals Dam was the fifth-largest dam in the United States.

But no amount of facts and figures will ever surmount the scorn voiced by generations of River People when referring to Bull Shoals Dam and the Army Corps of Engineers that built it. The irony that resulted from the "Flood Control Act," as untold numbers of Arkansans living near the gargantuan project were flooded out, their homes destroyed, is not lost. When Bull Shoals Dam finally came online in 1952, the downstream water temperature of the White River plunged so that the plentiful mussels—and the flourishing button trade they supported—declined to extinction. So did several native species of fish. As a side note, and to return to official reports archived with the *Encyclopedia of Arkansas History and Culture*:

> At completion, the project cost an estimated $86 million…the dam and reservoir immediately began to affect the local economy. Media coverage attracted attention to the region and resulted in the quick growth of the tourist industry. In 1940, there were only thirteen businesses that provided overnight accommodations. By 1970, 300 such establishments could be found. Assessed taxable real estate values, per capita income, and manufacturing payroll rose dramatically in the following decades. The area also now supports a retirement community.

L.C. Brown promised that he would wait until after John's death to reveal the secret location of Helen's grave. In 1979, John Black died and was buried in the nameless graveyard in St. Charles. More than a decade passed before L.C. decided that it was time to tell Helen's story. L.C.'s wife, Anna Grace, passed away in 1991. He found his thoughts turning more and more to the promise he made to John. After considering long and hard, L.C. knew that he wanted a proper marker for Helen's grave (in addition to the cedar tree). He also wanted a pardon for Helen from the governor of Arkansas, in order to clear the Spence name. In 2010, after the *Encyclopedia of Arkansas History and Culture* published the biographical entry on Helen Spence, L.C. noticed that DeWitt's Essex Funeral Home had placed a small metal marker at the grave of Cicero Spence, next to Helen's cedar tree. The marker had been in storage since 1930.

Whenever L.C. Brown tells the story, questions arise. People ask why L.C. promised to wait until after John was dead before telling. Some wonder why John himself never told where Helen was buried. Was it because John and Helen were lovers? Folks even go so far as to speculate on what might have happened if L.C. had died without telling anyone. Such impertinence tends to gall L.C., who is known to respond in exasperation, "Then nobody but God would've known where she was!"

"John Black just wanted someone to tell Helen's true story," L.C. explains for the umpteenth time. "John says to me, 'Hell, Brown, I figure if anybody could do it, it would be you.' John and Helen were not lovers. They's just buddies, is all. Ain't you ever had a buddy?'"

Epilogue

I have always admired natural beauty—a wonder existing unto itself, without artifice, needing no confirmation. Whether the form taken is human or animal, flora or fauna, sculpture, song or poem, makes no difference—as an action, revealing itself across time through steadfast courage and love.

The willful destruction of beauty is a damnable act. As I finish writing this in memoriam to Helen Ruth Spence (during the most verdant spring in years), the small waterside community of Mayflower, Arkansas, is being destroyed. A historic first, as it turns out.

The Mayflower I knew was a place of lush wetlands with a large lake popular among fishermen, home to waterlilies, trees, fish and birds, as well as peaceful families. Now it lies in ruin, its people sickened and the land, water and air saturated by oily chemicals due to the wealthiest name in the world: Exxon Mobil.

Just as with the first Great Depression, when the largest and richest grew monstrous while the smallest and poorest starved, now comes an era of overreach and revelatory action. People, wildlife, land and water exist at the mercy of a manmade machine pumping poison through leaky pipes running beneath every stream, lake and river. Just as it is all the same water, it is but one machine.

Exxon Mobil's broken, poisonous snake of pipeline crosses the White River; a river designated in 2013 a national treasure. This past January, the federal government proclaimed the White River watershed a "National Blueway." Encompassing one-third of Arkansas (17.8 million acres) the

"National Blueway" designation was promptly rejected by a citizen-led outcry over property rights. The U.S. Department of Interior rescinded the designation due to this groundswell of opposition.

Whether opposition to the broken oil pipeline will bring similar results remains an open question. The madness of greed at the expense of life-giving waters devours life itself, while the wheels of commerce flatten and grind. Fueled by the engine of the state, the result is Moloch, that ancient idol to whom burning children were sacrificed.

Helen Spence refused to "cow down," as we say in Arkansas. The machine that sought to defame and destroy her failed its group mission. No prison could hold her. Her truth shines, undimmed by the illusion of time.

About the Author

D enise White Parkinson was born, raised and educated in Arkansas. She attended college on scholarship and is a 1986 graduate of Hendrix College in Conway. Her career in journalism includes writing for the *Arkansas Democrat, Arkansas Democrat-Gazette, Arkansas Times, Mature Arkansas* news monthly, *Little Rock Free Press, Encyclopedia of Arkansas History and Culture, Memphis Flyer* and *Cooper-Young Lamplighter*. Since 2008, she has been the lead writer for *Hot Springs Life and Home* magazine. She resides in Hot Springs with

Photo by Leonard Stern.

her husband and children, where her proudest achievement is founding Hot Springs Area Community Gardens Network.

Printed in the USA
CPSIA information can be obtained
at www.ICGtesting.com
LVHW072151150823
755381LV00042B/1203